The Art of
Contemplation

OTHER BOOKS BY MARY ANGELON YOUNG

As It Is: A Year on the Road with a Tantric Teacher (2000)

Under the Punnai Tree, A Biography of Yogi Ramsuratkumar (2003)

Caught in the Beloved's Petticoats (2007)

Enlightened Duality—Essays on Art, Beauty, Life and Reality As It Is, with Lee Lozowick (2009)

The Baul Tradition—Sahaj Vision East & West (2014)

Krishna's Heretic Lovers, a novel (2014)

The Company of Avalon, a novel (2020)

The Queen's Tale, a novel (2021)

The Art of
Contemplation

Mary Angelon Young

HOHM PRESS
Chino Valley, Arizona

© 2021 Mary Angelon Young

Cover Design: Hohm Press

Interior Design and Layout: Becky Fulker, Kubera Book Design, Prescott, Arizona

ISBN: 978-1-942493-64-8
E-BOOK: 978-1-942493-65-5

Library of Congress Control Number: 2021932065

Hohm Press
P.O. Box 4410
Chino Valley, AZ 86323
800-381-2700
http://www.hohmpress.com

Photo Credits: Photos on pages 52 and 84 by Mary Angelon Young. Photo by Thomas Raffaele Young on page 34 of the Calanais Standing Stones on the Isle of Lewis, Outer Hebrides, Scotland with the author and her son, Zachary Dylan Parker.

This book was printed in the U.S.A. on recycled, acid-free paper using soy ink.

For everyone.

Acknowledgements

Thanks to my friend Regina Sara Ryan, editor of Hohm Press, who championed this book and gave ample space for my creative process to flourish. I'm deeply grateful to my husband, Thomas Raffaele Young, who endured my churning intensity as this book really began to take on a life of its own and demanded its due, and who read the manuscript for me and made essential contributions through his clarity of context and simplicity. Thank you, Paula Sarvani, for carefully proofreading the manuscript, as you have with so many of my books, and Clelia Lewis for help with the Index.

The "Contemplation of the Five Elements" has been inspired by my friend, Ayurvedic physician Dr. Robert Svoboda; his teachings and life of practice are sources of wisdom and solace for me. Many other countless individuals and friends, books and podcasts have inspired and nourished my experience of contemplation. To all, and in particular to my spiritual teacher, Lee Lozowick, and the revered saint, Yogi Ramsuratkumar, I offer deep bows of gratitude.

Contents

I

Taking Shelter

The key to what we miss and secretly long for is hidden within us.
—Michael Meade

Come, my friends,
Tis not too late to seek a newer world...
—Alfred Lord Tennyson

In reality there is nothing but the one moment all along.
Just as one single tree contains numberless trees, innumerable leaves,
infinite movement, and untold static states, so does one moment
contain an infinite number of moments, and within all these
countless moments lies the one single moment. Look, there is
motion as well as rest in that supreme moment.

—Anandamayi Ma

Contemplation is a road with no beginning and no end, taken from anywhere and everywhere that we find ourselves in life. *The Art of Contemplation* is intended to inspire your own inner journey, as I share some of mine and explore the treasure cache of contemplation, the reasons we truly need it, and how to work with the obstacles encountered along the way.

This book was written during the global pandemic of 2020, when the gravity of our situation called us, as individuals, to stay calm in the midst of chaos. Sheltering in place, or "confinement" as some prefer, we entered into a fierce and strange new world that demanded our sanity and inner strength. If we had not actively developed a contemplative side before this, the insistent, benevolent voice of that inner world, so famously avoided in today's society, now sounded a clarion call.

While political, cultural and religious structures crumble and we ride the roller coaster of ecological calamity, Mother Nature has brought a pandemic to remind us that she rules supreme. As humans struggle, the Earth goes on in the vast web of space-time, in sync with the precision movements of a solar system at home in a glorious galaxy. At the time of writing this introduction, the summer solstice of 2020 has passed, giving me the opportunity to contemplate nature, a recurring theme of this book, and how the days grow slowly shorter as the planet turns toward the autumn equinox.

Reliably, the dawn comes early this time of year in the high desert where I live. Each moment brings a change as the night is transfigured by dusky silver light that seeps in slowly and chases away the shadows. Soon enough, the sun crests the eastern mountaintop and the sky brightens to blue behind a screen of filmy clouds. The welcome cool of the night lingers and the air is fresh, with a bare tinge of moisture that will soon evaporate in the scorching heat of the sun.

Mornings are always a great time for contemplation, though it's really an all-day love affair as the light changes from hour to hour and the activities of the day roll along. Unlike formal meditation practice, in which one takes an intentional sitting posture and remains still for a period of time to go inward, in contemplation the body and mind can be still or active. Like meditation, contemplation spans a wide range of possibilities, but who can really say exactly what it is?

THE INNER WORLD

Contemplation is the timeless way to get in touch with our own intuition and deeper depths. My heavy, tattered dictionary (still used, despite Google, Ecosia, and Bing) says that to contemplate is "to look at thoughtfully, to pay attention and ponder, to dwell upon at length, to investigate, meditate upon, plunge into." A love of words and their etymology always invites me to go deeper, to the hidden meanings at the roots of language. In this case, contemplation comes from the Latin word *contemplatio,* meaning *the space one creates for observing auguries.*

This intrigues me. First of all, I look to the meaning of the old-fashioned word "auguries," which are the signs, omens, prophecies or foretellings that arise in the art of divination. And that's another word that evolved from Latin—"to divine" means to know by radical intuition. Today when we encounter an augury, we might think of it as a premonition, a lucky hunch, or we notice a synchronicity and recognize it as a sign in some way. Sometimes auguries occur in dreams. Maybe we have an astrology reading or cast the *I Ching*, hoping to get a take on a decision we have to make. In these classic arts of divination we seek wisdom and divine knowledge, but often we forget that what we seek is already inside ourselves.

And "the space one creates"? This one simple phrase is fertile ground for exploration. It links me right away to the five elements—earth, water, fire, air and space—and points directly to space, the original or mother element. The Western perspective recognizes four elements, but we'll delve into the Indian tradition of five elements and space in particular, because opening up to inner space is essential, not only to the contemplative or meditative moment, but also to the well-being of our whole person. We can begin the journey by allowing ourselves the space and time—the contemplative template—to explore our own outer and inner reality.

Definitions may point the way, but the contemplative mood is hard to pin down because it happens in the unlimited, expansive space inside. While it reveals its magic in ways that are unique and particular to your inner world, it also connects you with a universal experience of life. Most importantly, contemplation helps you to discover what is real and what is unreal by showing and revealing *reality as it is*.

A DIRECT EXPERIENCE

Contemplation develops a larger capacity for awareness and for being grounded in the present moment, connecting us directly with what is real in an increasingly unreal human world. Rooted in the reality of *what is* right now, it is a direct and immediate experience of life in an intimate meeting with yourself.

Whether we are engaged in activity or sitting quietly and doing nothing, a relationship with the inner world is developed through awareness that is focused in the present. Within this moment, contemplation can resolve the famous conflict between "doing and being," bringing this dichotomy together in a harmonious play. Of course, this demands some work on our part. Being present to both inner and outer simultaneously is not necessarily easy, but anything really worthwhile seldom is. We can develop a capacity for paying attention with inner stillness in all kinds of activities, from washing the dishes and sweeping the floor, to handling the business of the day, attending a meeting, reading to a child, writing a memoir or playing music.

Though we have heard many times that the present moment is where healing power actually resides, this is an idea that becomes real to us when we make it our own. An intellectual grasp is a good beginning, and yet to tap the power of the present we must experiment and discover the truth for ourselves. It's through our direct experience of reality that we verify for ourselves the truth of the wisdom we receive from traditional sources and the world around us. How liberating to taste a rare moment, through direct experience, in which the depths are serene even when the surface is rippled by wind or lashed by storms!

"Mindfulness" is another familiar concept, made popular through the panorama of Buddhist meditation teachings widely available in the contemporary world. I like the simple term "paying attention," which is similar to mindfulness. When our attention is present, we can see what is going on inside and outside simultaneously, a practice that opens enormous vistas of insight.

If you're new to contemplation or needing to renew your contemplative life, you'll want to make distinctions about what does or does not support you to be centered in yourself and at home in your own inner culture. You'll probably need to carve out or "steal" a little time when you can relax and be free, at least for the moment, from appointments, deadlines and the hurried needs of the day. You may choose to turn off your cell phone or leave it in airplane mode when you are yearning for a contemplative mood to re-charge your vital energy.

Some of my friends now schedule one device-free day a week, especially those who have children and teenagers. Look to see for yourself if that pressing online task can wait. Send that email later! It's not about procrastination; it's about being aware of how you use your time and energy, and giving yourself the gift of a much-needed moment with you. As contemplation becomes a palpable and real state of being, it will carry you through, like a surfer on a wave.

TRUE NATURE

History tells a bleak story of how the survival imperatives of human beings (that reptilian part of the brain) have propelled us collectively toward violence, greed, war and division. At the same time, human beings have produced beautiful and profound art, philosophy and science because we are essentially designed to self-reflect. As we learn more about the interconnectivity within nature, today's science is showing us that—though conflict and the drive to survive exists—underlying all is a foundation principle of co-operation and mutuality. How desperately we need to shift toward allowing these patterns to awaken and emerge in humanity. It's a revolution that happens one person at a time.

All spiritual quests sooner or later lead to contemplation because it is both natural and necessary to the evolution of a human being. Once we are pointed toward our own transformation, the mood of contemplation arises from a natural impulse toward introspection, for the moment of stillness within, for an emptying out so that we may receive anew and gain access to the original self—the true nature that exists within. It's an organic process, just as bud goes to flower and flower goes to seed, which drops to the ground to begin another round of creation. In this very natural way, contemplation may grow into spontaneous states of meditation or prayer, essential practices found in every spiritual path. For some of us this may include profound mystical experiences, while for others the ordinary simplicity of daily life becomes profound and fulfilling.

These internal states might be called stillness, calm abiding, or the practice of pure awareness—or even "inner yoga," as yoga is anything that links us to the Divine. It does not matter what we call it. What does matter is that we, as human beings, evolve in a reciprocal love affair with the Universe from which we are created in love. As we contemplate our own existence within the mystery of Life, we begin to expand as vessels of transformation, which benefits all beings. A great generosity of awareness comes to live with us, and our contemplation takes flight.

As I spiral through the themes of this book, weaving and interweaving the threads then looping back again, let your mind and heart be open. Now and then, drop your plans and business of the day and just be present. Since this book has found its way into your hands, you'll probably find much that is familiar and affirming. At the same time, perhaps you'll find new and creative ways to explore your own art of contemplation. Let your intuitive awareness be inspired as you read. Be curious without drawing conclusions. Clearing the slate of the mind, letting go of the burden of fixed certainty, we can cultivate the inner freedom to un-know what we think we know. It's a beautiful marriage of confidence, trust, and simple presence that paves the way into moods of contemplation, free of concepts and rules.

The experience of sheltering in place during this pandemic continues to open into a powerful and challenging new world.

In many ways the word "sheltering" speaks for how we can take refuge within ourselves to ponder the contemplative side of life. Relaxing into receptive inner space, we rejuvenate and restore, tap into intrinsic healing, intuitive and creative energies, know things in unexpected ways. There, at the level of source water, the river of life flows pristine, and we may even touch the ineffable. The Taoists have a beautiful way of expressing it. Lao Tzu said, "Muddy water, let stand, becomes clear." Clarity is one of the many gifts of contemplation, and as we build a capacity for the inner journey, a sacred world is revealed in the mirror of the soul.

"The mirror of the sky reflects my soul."
Baul song

II

Sacred World

The forests and our lives are connected and interconnected in ways we can only wonder about. Sometimes science walks in and answers.
—Diana Beresford-Kroeger

The stars, the sun, and the moon are never impatient
Silently, they follow the stream of pure Existence
—Baul song

Knowing that you love the earth changes you, activates you to depend and protect and celebrate. But when you feel that the earth loves you in return, that feeling transforms the relationship from a one-way street into a sacred bond.
—Robin Wall Kimmerer

We are surrounded by the sacred; it is in the core of our being and in the Earth's. It is the essential nature of everything that is. The "sacred" is not something religious, or even spiritual. It is not a quality we need to learn or to develop. It belongs to the primary nature of all that is.
—Llewellyn Vaughan-Lee

The earliest sacred text of India, the Rig Veda, tells us that we must contemplate the vast space of the sky in order to know our true nature. Embedded as we are in the limitations of the Western mindset, it might be easy to miss the magic and power of this instruction. Aren't we beyond such simple advice? After all, it was thousands of years ago when the *rishis* and *rishikas,* those ancient diviners and sages, perceived the nature of reality that is transmitted through the Vedas. How could they understand the complex reality of surviving in the twenty-first century?

Such utter simplicity makes this ancient wisdom sound almost facile, when in fact it is simple but not easy. Turning to nature to remember our own intrinsic being is a challenge to our busy lives, ruled by our devices and the endeavor to survive in these difficult times. It also opposes the deep-seated cultural belief that we must dominate and conquer nature—a worldview that has led to the dying of our planet's oceans, the melting of the polar caps, the burning of the rain forests, and rapacious felling of old growth trees. For some, finding the sacred in the natural world may confront a dwindling faith in the basic goodness of life.

Indigenous elders, spiritual leaders, scientists, healers in all fields, and ecologists have joined their voices to plead for a renewal of humanity's connection with the Earth and the natural wisdom that our remote ancestors carried and lived. Hearing the cries of the Earth, many of us have realized that today's urgent problems can only be grappled with effectively if human beings reclaim a rightful place in the life of our planet. The alternative may be to die as a species in the world of our making.

Spending time in nature in simple ways can immediately open up a neglected relationship with Mother Earth—walking under autumn trees or down dusty desert paths, watching the phases of the moon, digging the earth to plant a garden, taking in an expanse of water and basking in sun, sand and fresh air, or hiking a mountain trail that opens into distant vistas. It's really a process of remembering and attuning with what is already present.

Gazing at the sky connects us to what is real and actually can be a form of yoga that awakens the heart to a deep sense of connectedness within the vast play of life. Contemplating that unfathomable space can inspire greater simplicity in our lives. It can help to clear out the attics and basements and closets of our stuffed-full psyches, bombarded as we are with information and images and personal history—some of it painful, all of it congested with the tidal wash of flotsam and jetsam accumulated over a lifetime. In the process we begin to glimpse the true nature the ancient ones are telling us about.

HOLY PRESENCE

Through contemplation we grow our capacity to pay attention with a sensory experience of here and now. As our awareness expands, the reality of the present moment emerges as one of the most precious gifts that we receive from the natural world.

Nature is always happening here and now. The rain is falling... now. The rain has stopped falling...now. The sun is shining. The clouds have covered the sun. The wind is blowing in gusts that rattle the windows. The wind has calmed and the air is still. This simple approach to noticing and acknowledging *what is* actually cultivates the simplicity and awareness of contemplation.

Holy presence permeates all of nature and communicates the sacred. The ancient Celts had a profound understanding of the magical world of nature and how subtle dimensions of reality come through in a particular and strong way in certain "thin places." In the thin places, the veils between spirit and matter, between this world and the eternal world, are as evanescent as gossamer, providing a passageway for beings to traverse the realms.

As a traveler and pilgrim, I've experienced the sacred in this way walking amidst the standing stones of Scotland, Ireland and Brittany; pondering ocean tides on wind-swept beaches around the world, or awestruck by the sentient power of trees, like the magnificent redwoods of California, the soaring firs in the Black Forest of Germany, the aspen groves of Colorado, the old cherry trees of France, and the punnai, mango and tamarind trees of India.

In recent years studies have documented how walking in forests, and especially under tall trees, relieves anxiety and fear. Trees give shelter in many ways and can be amazingly empathetic. As a tree climber, many of my childhood mornings were spent held in the arms of the flowering magnolia in my grandmother's back yard or playing beneath the venerable spreading oaks of Louisiana and Arkansas, where I grew up. Trees still teach me how to be contemplative, how to recognize and access the sanctuary I need.

I've felt exalted in the pure presence of lochs, waterfalls and meandering streamlets in Scotland. The sacred canyons of Arizona and Utah have uplifted and humbled me just as much as the Mississippi River or the mighty Ganges, the lush jungles and bodhi tree shrines of India. Here, in my mile-high desert home, piñon and juniper speak to me, the brilliant night sky is the friend of my soul.

It's the communion with nature in these experiences that has been transformative and sustaining for me. When we approach with respect, empathy and even reverence, the holy presence of nature becomes vivid, alive and intimate. Listening deeply, we hear the sound of our Mother's voice. Resting, relaxing, sinking into calmness and inner space, it's "a mother and child reunion," to quote the songwriter Paul Simon. *Let your mind wander to remember when, where, how you've known the thin places over the years.*

THE METAPHORS OF NATURE

There is a reason why we call her "Mother Nature." We cry and laugh upon her breast. We are born from her substance; our substance will die back into hers. My love affair with nature began as a small child, when I was captivated by trees, plants, flowers, mud, sand, birds, insects and animals. Weather intrigued me, especially thunderstorms and tornadoes. There were four distinct seasons where I grew up, each one with its unique wonders, especially as the leaves turned to the colors of flame. In summer I loved the mimosa trees with their sweet-smelling feathery pink flowers that tickled my face. I could play for hours in the shade of the black walnut trees, under the calla lilies, or swinging on wisteria vines.

In the early seventies I went to live with my young son in an alternative community deep in the Buffalo River watershed in the Ozark Mountains. There we swam in pristine blue-green water, ran free in the woods, discovered rare wild magnolias and tiny orchids, patches of healing goldenseal and wild ginseng. My love of nature expanded naturally to organic gardening, which taught me a new form of contemplation in holy labor. Living in the remote Ozarks for six years, I discovered profound metaphors in nature's cycles and patterns as well as in her sheer beauty. During those years I considered the Earth to be my spiritual teacher. I was learning from the goddess herself.

Now I live in the high desert. Coming from a green world to the austere, rugged beauty of the desert was an adjustment. It took many years to grow my capacity to see the magic of the dry lands, where the sun's power burns bright. In the process, my concept of "beauty" morphed and got as big as the desert sky. Most nights before bed, I go outside to contemplate the universe. Sometimes the sky is opaque, thick with clouds, impenetrable. At other times, the same dark sky is the thrilling diamond spread of the Milky Way. Nature, the great metaphor, comes softly home. This is real. This is the way it is. Whether I see clouds or stars, behind it all is a vast mystery—steady, eternal, formless, unchanged, always present, with vast space connecting it all together.

Bringing awareness to the element of space opens the mind, expands perspective and connects me to the reality of the other four elements as they intermingle in infinite creative forms. Nature reveals her powers in countless ways. In the desert every rock is a study in weight, shape, texture. The songs of birds, the scurrying flash of a lizard just awakened from winter's sleep, the return of the hummingbirds after their arduous spring migration, the profuse mounds of wild purple verbena that come up by surprise in my herb garden, or the coming of a summer storm—all of these wonders nourish me.

The raw beauty of nature uplifts and restores me. Her ruthless, inexorable processes and cycles have taught me secrets of continuity—how life endures through death and renewal. Nature helps me to see and know what is real, what is true. She shows me the blueprint of existence in the patterns of life, with its threads of connection and the unity of oneness underlying all. Within her wild diversity exists a vast array of resonant symbols that tell the stories of life and speak to some of our most essential human questions—how to live and how to die, as well as how to be reborn.

Observing and pondering the patterns and cycles in nature builds a capacity for resilience in me. Nature helps me trust in the basic goodness of life's deepest intention, even in the deadly viruses that wreak havoc upon humankind. Despite our trials and tribulations in the human world, life does go on, and its magnificent, impersonal splendor soothes and inspires me because it is real. I can lean into and trust its reliable realness.

The Divine Artist creates these infinite forms of gorgeous, impermanent yet enduring beauty that touch my heart. I'm not the only writer who seeks beauty and is inspired to write about it. Many if not most of us who create art of any kind are inspired by the beauty of nature in one way or another, because the contemplative arts, when followed into their depths, can open the doors of the heart to reality as it is. *While you're reading, take a moment to stop and notice something in nature that is beautiful to you. Then go to your laptop or your journal and describe it...or sketch it, weave it, dance it or sing it. Let yourself freely express your eloquence and wordcraft, your love of movement, your passion for color and form.*

CONTEMPLATION OF THE FIVE ELEMENTS

Following one thread in the rich tapestry of India's wisdom traditions—described in the philosophical teachings of Samkhya, Vastu and Ayurveda—let's consider the five elements from which everything is made. Earth is grounding in mountains, dirt, sand, mud. Water is as soothing in the bathroom shower as it is in lakes and streams and oceans. Fire inspires awe and creative vision, even in a candle flame. Air is the source of the *prana*, or life force, that we breathe in every moment. Space is everywhere. As the matrix or mother element, space is expansive, connecting us to everything and everyone. All five elements are intermingled; if we contemplate one of the elements, it will lead to the others.

The five elements of our sacred world mesmerize and uplift, each in their own way, inspiring poetry and praise. They draw us in through their creations and speak to us because we too are made of them. They are, literally and symbolically, the foundation of our own physical being, which makes them refreshing, restorative, healing. The five elements taking form as Mother Nature have no personal history, no cultural, social or religious overlay but are essentially holy, free and sacred. As the origins of life, they resonate in the depths of our own being. *Feel into the elements as you read the following contemplation slowly, silently or aloud to yourself. Pause as often as you wish. Take your time. Do as much as you wish at any sitting. Come back to it often.*

Contemplating Space. We begin with space, the mother element, out of which the other four elements arise. Space is everywhere. I am located in space. It's right in front of my face as I write or raise my hand—through space—to take the cup of coffee that sits on my desk. It's the awesome expanse between me and the raw hulking mountain across the canyon from where I sit at my desk looking out a large window that faces north. Upon its rocky, rugged flank, the pine trees wave in the wind. I am connected to their movement, their existence and joy, through space. *Look around you now, take in the space of your own environment.*

In this expansive mood, I take refuge in the human bond I share with those who are near to my heart, with friends both old and new, with people I've never met all over the world. Even if we are miles apart right now, wherever we take shelter at this powerful time of challenge and change, we are connected through space. My heart traverses the unseen currents of space to touch the hearts of those I love. Prayer for the well-being of us all follows on wings of gold. *Take a moment now and invite your heart to open to your loved ones. Feel your connection with them, wherever they are.*

The mother element, space or *akasha*, is related to our individual sense of hearing and sound. We can tune into space by bringing awareness to how sound moves through apparent emptiness as we listen, speak, sing or play an instrument. Notice how words dance as melody or a single note sounds itself in pure space. This applies to all music and all use of words. (With gratitude to the goddess Saraswati, patroness of the arts of speech, of music, of writing).

When we write words on paper (and digital words on our laptops), we are exploring our own inner space. Poetry is a unique arrangement of words in space. Often, it's what is not said but implied through the space between the words that makes a poem or a piece of writing touch us. Contemplate space by exploring the vast space within and without. It may lead you to *sukha*, the word that Sanskrit scholar Robert Svoboda translates as "good space." *Rest for a moment here, within yourself. Sense the space.*

Contemplating Air. The air element is experienced through the sense of touch. In feeling the caress of breeze or wind, you can become aware of how the air holds you. I walk outside the door and the same wind that moves the pine trees on the mountains now makes tendrils of hair play upon my cheek.

When you focus on your breath, you are relating with air. *Prana* or life force comes to us through the air we breathe. Attention to the breath immediately connects us to what is real and grounds us in the body, encouraging the circulation of *prana* through organs, blood, bones and cells. Just paying attention to the breath is a powerful opening into a contemplative or meditative mood and is automatically enlivening, uplifting and calming.

Pause and pay attention to your breath, without doing anything to fix or change it. Just notice the rhythm, where it catches, is strained or shallow. Be with your breath as it comes and goes, whether it's easy and full or ragged and tense. Now shift just slightly to breathe intentionally, inhaling and exhaling through your nose in as full and steady a way as you can. Keep breathing in this way for a few minutes, letting yourself become intimate with your breath.

Contemplating Fire. This primal element not only gives us light, and therefore the sense of sight and our ability to see the manifest world, but also spiritual vision, creative inspiration and the power to transform. We are warmed by fire, physically, emotionally and spiritually. Our digestion is a fire; our anger is a fire. Our love is a fire. You can be intimate with fire by meditating upon the glorious sun and how its healing rays penetrate and warm your body.

Sunlight on my eyelids, taken in through the open palms of my hands, or absorbed by the length of the spine when I lay in the sun on my belly, causes the inner light to surge within. Moonlight is a pale, soft fire that can heal and inspire; the light of the stars ignites our yearning in deep ways. Contemplate fire to expand the spiritual vision that cultivates faith and a connection to what is true and everlasting.

Gazing at a candle flame is a simple way to relate with the element of fire. We work with fire when we're cooking on a gas stove, building and tending a fire in a wood stove, or sitting with friends around a bonfire. The traditional Vedic religion of India is based upon fire worship through a sacred fire—a *homa* fire or *dhuni*. If your circumstance allows you to build a small, well-tended, contained fire outside (being vigilant about sparks flying and aware of the serious dangers of fire), you can experience your own version of a dhuni fire. Sit at the fire and tend it, one small stick at a time, as you offer something that is meaningful to you. Flowers or petals make good offerings. So does the resin of pine tree, sage, sweet herbs of all kinds, and ghee (clarified butter). Words or prayers written on paper and even drops of water can go into the flames. With intention, we can offer up our obstacles, troubles, doubts, negative patterns, the baggage we carry from the past to be transmuted by the power of fire. Or, we can simply express gratitude for all that has been given. *How are you transformed by fire?*

Contemplating Water. Science tells us that our bodies are mostly water, the source of life on Earth. Water is ubiquitously present in our moment-to-moment experience as the sense of taste and the blood in our veins. Water is also present in our changing moods and in the state of creative flow. Water moves inside us as felt states such as joy, gratitude, happiness or sorrow, grief, fear, revulsion. The water element is present in our empathy with others, in our ability to blend and harmonize. The water element as pure mood informs melody, music and poetic speech. Water gives life to leaves and petals and shines in the moist eyes of night owls.

Water is everywhere, even in the desert—although for me there is nothing that compares with standing on the shore of a river or ocean. The vast grandeur and pure elemental power of the ocean is as comforting and nourishing as it is exhilarating and terrifying. Like fire and air, just as water gives life, she also has the power to destroy.

Every kind of water has its own mood or *rasa* (a Sanskrit word meaning "nectar, flavor or taste") and communication, whether it is an ocean, sea, lake, stream, rivulet, oasis pool or forest spring. We can give thanks to the water element every time we drink a glass, take a shower or bath, enjoy the rain, watch the clouds, or make and eat a nourishing soup. We can appreciate water every time we look at a tree or another human being. Without water there is no life. *Use these reflections to feel and express your gratitude for water.*

Contemplating Earth. The earth element is associated with the sense of smell, which has amazing power to alter your mood. Most spiritual traditions use incense of various kinds to invoke the sacred through the sense of smell. Sandalwood is known throughout the world as a spiritually potent aromatic that can help invoke a meditative or contemplative mood. The scents of sage, mint, or evergreens like pine and cedar can uplift and clear the mind, while lavender is calming. The fragrance of an heirloom rose, spring hyacinths or wisteria blossoms inspire with their sweetness. The rot of a dead mouse in the attic, the earthy decay of the compost pile, the stench of industrial toxins are equally evocative and will invariably induce another kind of mood altogether.

Attuning to the earth element we become more stable and grounded. We become aware of our roots and foundations. Bringing awareness to our bones and connecting those bones with the rocky elemental bones of the Earth is a potent way to steady and root ourselves in what is real. When you sit, feel how your bones connect with chair, floor, earth, stone ledge or cushion.

Contemplation while walking is a powerful earth grounding, as our feet stand and move upon the firm substance of the earth. We can walk and sit upon the earth with awareness, appreciation and reverence. Every hill, crystal, flower, bud, leaf, insect, dog, cat, elephant and mud hole can remind us of the earth element. Earth is present in the food we eat, the car we drive (metal, of course, comes from deep in the earth), the stony mountains, the dirt paths, the gravel or paved road, the gemstones we wear and adore. *Relax, sink into the strong foundations of the Earth, sense your own roots, your grounded connection to her.*

CYCLES OF CHANGE

The metaphors of nature open me to deeper symbols of reality as it is, prepare me to roll with ongoing change as well as with the totally unexpected, mysterious and irrational. The symbolism of the wild helps me accept and even embrace the three forces that move all of life: creation, preservation and destruction. In the Sanskrit traditions these forces are called the *gunas*. The ancient Celts have an image that depicts these three forces, with each one flowing into the next. It's called the *triskelion*, and it's a powerful symbol of constant transformation, which is what life is all about. The ancients knew and lived by this wisdom, because they knew that the one thing we can count on is change. Everything dies, everything is reborn. Energy manifest in matter is in a constant state of transformation.

The raw, primal wildness of nature is an ever-changing mirror that helps me see the epic of my own journey and the reality of my inevitable death as a transition to another state of being. In a culture where death is denied and feared at every turn, courting this kind of knowledge is a pearl of great price. In this way nature can help us prepare for our own death.

In the sanctuary of Triveni where I live, my cottage is surrounded by high desert wilderness. Walking is one of my favorite activities and a great time for contemplation. It's not uncommon to come across the shed skin of rattlesnakes or the snake itself, an immediate reminder of death and the great transformation from one state to another. Everywhere I look there are trees, bushes and plants in every possible stage of birth, life, death, renewal, rebirth. The skeletons of trees long dead are the favorite perches of the birds, from which they survey their winged and feathered domain. Ravens, mockingbirds, doves, orioles, and even the tiny, zooming hummingbirds become still and seemingly contemplative sitting at the top of the stark, weathered remains of a particular pine near my cottage.

Agave is the mandala of the high desert. The Aztecs revered this life-giving plant as the goddess Mayahuel, a feminine divinity with the power to heal and sustain, from which potent or sweet elixirs are distilled (agave syrup and tequila). The agaves are always "works in progress"—some are in their once-in-a-lifetime phase of the magnificent, towering stalk that blooms in clusters of small flowers, after which the whole plant quickly dies. Others are small rosettes (called "pups") popping up near a healthy parent plant that grows out of the rotting remains of its own parent or ancestor. It's all happening at once.

An avid watcher of stars and the phases of the moon, I contemplate the big sky of the desert world, with its movement of clouds, wind and rain. Glorious rain! Here in the high desert, everyone eagerly awaits the arrival of the summer monsoon that will bring relief from the windy, dry heat of May and June. This year, we are well into September and still the rains have not come, which some say is yet another sign of climate change. The heat becomes merciless as the sun sears all tender things, including humans. Even the bobcats and coyotes slink about searching for a drink or a shaded place, their fur sparse and ragged from shedding.

What a release when the rains finally come! The desert prairie and mesas turn green, as the plant world—in suspended animation in the brutal dry heat—now springs to action in heroic growing spurts. I can almost hear the shout of joy that emanates from the natural world when the rain arrives. The summer that tormented us is suddenly transformed into a wondrous playground of lovely downpours, shifting cloud cathedrals shafted with gold and silver light, torrential cloudbursts and blue curtains of rain on distant mountain landscapes, delicious winds that play across the prairie, sweeping up to the mesa to wave the sturdy limbs of wet, glistening pines in a dance of delight. All this is ornamented by the sudden appearance of fleeting beauty in ephemeral, awe-inspiring rainbows.

In an ever-changing cosmos, Neowise, the comet that blazed across the sky in the spring and early summer of 2020, has come and gone. While it was here, the comet spoke to a primordial place in my psyche and reverberated in my DNA. It boggled my mind, in a good way, to realize that this comet has a cycle of return and will appear again in our world in 6,800 or so years. After Neowise came the Perseids, the shooting stars of August that come every year from the Perseus constellation deep in space.

What is changing in your life at this time? When we let go and take the dive, we just might free-float or soar effortlessly, like the golden eagles of the high desert. Moods, both sweet and tender or penetrating and challenging, will arise. Insight, awe, unexpected creative urges visit us, or we simply notice that we are more relaxed. We can face our fears and work with them. Our confusion suddenly lifts, and we have a clear knowing of which path to take. These gifts arrive unmediated by the usual mind when contemplatio's garden is well-tended.

THE EARTHY MYSTIC

Being present with the sacred world, we fall into a moment of contemplari, knowing that which is unknown in a radical intuition that is non-verbal and revelatory. It is a dance between body and soul, matter and spirit—a soulful marriage that intuits the Great Unknown. To *know* in this way, in a leap beyond the conditioned thinking mind, sets us free of rigid mindsets, dogmas, creeds and concepts all kinds. Even if it is only for this moment, we can un-know all that we think we know, which opens the mind and heart to the inner reserves of a much deeper knowledge, referred to as *buddhi* in the great Hindu scripture, the Bhagavad Gita.

Communing with nature, we are opened to the innate gifts of the soul. One of the twentieth-century saints of India, Neem Karoli Baba, voiced this vision of inclusivity when he said, "The best form to worship God is all forms." Contemplating nature we might discover that even the most pragmatic of us has an ordinary, earthy mystic sheltering somewhere within. Swami Ramdas of Kerala, India was a prolific writer, poet, and lover of the divine presence that he found embodied everywhere. He once wrote:

> *Mystics have a sense of beauty. The mystics are in tune with nature, and through nature with God. When they stand before the vastness of a landscape, the greenness of a forest, the scintillating expanse of the blue water of the ocean, the golden hue of the sunrise and sunset, they feel the hallowed presence of the Most High. In ecstasy they pour out their hearts in celestial rhapsodies and songs. They love solitude where they converse with God.*

The mystics of both East and West have been telling us this for thousands of years: it's all within you. Every person is made of stardust and carries the patterns of the Universe within. It's humbling to realize how infinitesimally tiny we are in the grandeur of life. There is nothing sentimental or glamorous about our earthy, ordinary mysticism. In this way, nature can help us learn humility.

In the bright, burning awareness of what is, a wordless "converse with God" may arise to take us beyond concept or form. Prayer, or presence, can be silent and still, thick with the power of intention, or it can be a fervent, powerful request of the Divine in words or conversation. It can come as a poem or in any creative act. It's an open field where we can run and play and create as we wish.

Still, many of us, especially Westerners, are skeptical, cynical or rational about prayer. We may have rejected all organized religion because we're turned off by the cruelties and abuse that religions have perpetrated upon humanity, or we've personally suffered abuse in the hands of its spiritual leaders. Opening up to what Thomas Merton called the "new seeds of contemplation," we can reclaim the sacred in life with prayers of our own making. We can discover spiritual presence in new, healing and wonderful ways. Mother Nature is a vital part of that journey.

Desert Song

simmered in the heat
of a clear and lovely night
the songs of wind and
early summer crickets
place me here, on holy ground
honoring the local gods
and the spirit of this land

the bones of dry hills
ring out in silence, they are
noble, daunting, proud
under the star-strewn night

a great peace descends,
hums with pleasure
basks in pure goodness
while the whispering wind
goes here and there,
calls and blesses,
messenger of the stars

III

Radical Contemplation

*The most radical thing any of us can do at this time
is to be fully present to what is happening in the world.*
—Joanna Macy

*Transformation at the level of the individual soul
generates the imagination and collective energy needed to
change the conditions of the world.*
—Michael Meade

*All beings, including each one of us, enemy and friend alike,
exist in patterns of mutuality, interconnectedness,
co-responsibility and ultimately in unity.*
—Roshi Joan Halifax

Today, as we negotiate the terrain of a vastly challenged Earth, we are in desperate need of a revolution that is inherently spiritual. The more we see the depth of suffering and the impossibly complex problems of the world, feelings of powerlessness and helplessness come up. How can we make a difference? It can be overwhelming, and yet, we begin where we are by simplifying and clarifying our own lives. My spiritual teacher often said that the transformation of consciousness happens one individual at a time. It's a teaching voiced by many wise ones, and it places a great responsibility—and possibility—upon each person. We all have work to do. It starts within then spreads out to the world around us.

AT THE HEART OF THE WORLD

Contemplation is a revolutionary act in which we travel intentionally in the opposite direction of the speeding, clamoring, competitive, madhouse world. We are going within. As a species we've had thousands of years during which the predatory side of humanity has dominated through war and violence. Today, in our lifetime, each one of us is called to the "spiritual and psychological integrity" that seeds and grows a personal transformation, which moves our species toward the recognition of essential oneness and connection. We have the blueprint within us, but we have to choose it, work with it, bring it to life. It's the embodiment of our ideals that will make a difference.

Growing up in the Deep South, the brutal inequity of a racially segregated culture burned at my heart as a child. As a teenager, the Civil Rights Movement further incited a radical view in me, and as I went away to college in the fall of 1968, the assassinations of Robert Kennedy and Martin Luther King shook the foundations of the world I was entering as a young person. My rebellion against the status quo was fueled by the sleeping lassitude and denial of my parents' generation, the greed and darkness in government leaders, the failure of the church to provide spiritual sustenance, the Vietnam war, and ongoing racial injustice. The poets of my generation spoke through the power of music, generating a revolutionary mood that spawned seekers of truth in all directions, including me. It was rock & roll, psychedelic journeys, and a mystical connection to nature that propelled the next phase in my coming of age.

By 1972, I was immersed in the growing hippie countercul-ture, where going "back to the land" was a form of protest and a spiritual quest. Six years in the mountain wilds of the Ozarks grounded me in an earth-based spirituality that included eco-feminist perspectives and my own search for God as Mother. Our intentional community was formed around a powerful, emerging awareness of the Earth's plight—even then, it was not hard to see alarming trends of greater ecological decline. Leaving behind the infrastructure of society and technological culture, we sought an alternative culture based on organic gardening and simple life-styles in tune with the Earth's rhythms. In our idealism, we created a land trust to protect the 520 acres of land where we lived—green mountains with high limestone bluffs, clear blue-green rivers, and gorgeous seasonal changes in the mostly deciduous forests—from being parceled and sold, stripped for lumber or mined. This first community experience was the seedbed of many experiences that would come later in my life.

For me there was no dichotomy between spiritual and political awareness, and by 1978 I had left that community to raise my son in the small mountain town of Fayetteville, Arkansas. Working with a natural-foods wholesale cooperative and swept into the feminist movement of the times, I became passionately involved in the struggle of the American Indian Movement (AIM) and indigenous tribes, who were fighting against the United States government to stop uranium mining and other abuses on tribal lands. In the dead of night, we delivered food, money and clothes off the back of our co-op trucks, to young Native American activists in Winslow, Arizona.

Traveling with a few women friends to the Pine Ridge Reservation of the Sioux Nation in South Dakota to hear activist-poet John Trudell speak was an unforgettable and profound experience that expanded my awareness, taking me as well to the land of the Cherokee in Oklahoma for rallies and concerts to benefit Native Americans like Rita Silk-Nauni and Leonard Peltier. These were life-changing moments, when I was extremely fortunate to support, in a small way, the ongoing struggle of indigenous people and all people of color for justice and dignity.

Those are little pieces of a long and complex story, better told in detail some other time, but it was an important stretch of the road that eventually led me to a radical contemplative life. By the mid-1980s, I was living in Boulder, Colorado and working on my master's degree in transpersonal psychology. As I became grounded in the teachings of Dr. C.G. Jung, my inner life was activated, especially in relationship with archetypes, myths, and the Divine Mother in her many forms and images. I began to sense that, for me, the best way to make a difference in the world was to work for change at the individual level. It was the fire of personal transformation that called to me, kindled to flame by the loss of my mother when I was thirty-six years old.

The feelings of loss and bereavement that followed her death catalyzed my spiritual path, which was soon charged with the super-fuel of meeting my spiritual teacher, Lee Lozowick, in 1987, and his master, the beloved south Indian saint, Yogi Ramsuratkumar, a few years later. Thus began many adventures over three decades of ashram life, meetings with modern sages and practitioners of many traditions, and becoming immersed in the disciplines of spiritual practice and self-study.

All along the way, my *sadhana* or spiritual path has included travel, giving me a big view of the awe-inspiring beauty of the world in all its grandeur and diversity. Discovering the spiritual treasures of India, I found a living mythology and a rich, all-inclusive divinity, both masculine and feminine, that resonated with the depths in me, inspiring my heart and imagination. At the same time, visiting the great cities of the world as well as spiritual communities, ashrams and temples, I saw firsthand the global degeneration and decay of human culture and ecosystems, especially poignant in India, where Western values and the rampant growth of technologies have been superimposed on sacred culture.

Over time my radical bent has grown prolifically in the seedbed of a contemplative life. Now, as I turn seventy, this long and winding way has delivered me into a universal view that makes me deeply aware of my oneness with everyone and everything. As the seeds of contemplation have ripened, the soul of the world has become tangible and real for me, making the silence or song of my inner life potent in ways that I cannot fathom. In my experience, whatever roads we have walked to arrive where we are now, contemplation will bring us to live at the heart of the world.

Miracle

captives of the unreal,
splayed upon the rocks of fear,
we are burning
tender shoots and leaves,
killing pale and sacred flowers

at the spectacle of our folly
sorrow seeps in
with no relief in sight,
nothing to do
but go deeper down
to the marrow of things,
pare away the festered flesh

to see how we could be
free in the moment
of our miracle

relics of star-crossed soul,
ancient as a petrified forest,
we are hard as rock crystal,
but melted down
to natural ecstasy
we are rich as butter and cream,
sweet as honey and syrup,
like sunrise in the mouth

THE GIFT OF A BROKEN HEART

Feeling the suffering in the world is a sure sign that we are called into contemplation. I'm grateful for the blessing and teachings I've received from my spiritual lineage, as well as from many other traditions of great-hearted individuals who have inspired me on the path. My teacher gave a speech in India in 1998 that has stayed with me through the years, in which he said: "My master, Yogi Ramsuratkumar, has given me the gift of a broken heart that only God can heal." Over the years, in deep moments when I endured loss, Lee advised me from his own experience, saying, "You need to have a broken heart that only God can heal." It's a universal teaching that speaks to everyone, especially at this crucial moment in time on Earth.

We are not strangers to heartbreak. It's deep, heavy, and often dark, with places that sink down into a seemingly bottomless well of sorrow. As scholar and spiritual teacher Dr. Thomas Hübl says, "We are born into a traumatized world." Every human being carries the trauma of the Earth as well as personal and/or collective trauma that begs to be acknowledged. If we are honest, a cumulative weight pulls at us, just below the surface of our busy lives and thought patterns. Many of us are struggling to survive, to care for children and aging parents. We wrestle with a personal health crisis, chronic pain, a divorce, a dislocation or financial worries. The terrible fact is that many people have nowhere to live and nothing to eat. We encounter the inevitable losses of aging, which are a unique and unavoidable call to contemplation. At any and all ages, we suffer when someone close to us dies, sometimes leaving our lives undone.

The circumstance of the world as it is today creates immense stress and conflict because, when one human being suffers, we all suffer; what the Earth suffers, we all suffer. We recoil from strangers and those we consider "other," who don't wear the right clothes or look "successful." We feel a grave distance from those who have a skin color or sexual preference or gender that is different from our own. Another form of division is created when we judge and condemn those we have labeled as the perpetrators of human suffering and the suffering of the Earth.

The path of contemplation asks us to see into how we are intermingled—what affects one impacts all. Even those who condone or perpetrate violence and avarice need our compassionate clarity (not our complicity, complacency or cynicism), and even our love, because their behaviors are symptoms of the deep suffering of the human soul. This does not mean that we don't protest the injustice and wrongs of society. Gandhi's life continues to inspire the nonviolent revolutionary spirit in me. But we also have to be the change that we want to see, taking up the revolutionary act of healing and working with ourselves through radical contemplation.

Covid-19 is one of the forces of heartbreak that charge through our world like the four horsemen of the apocalypse, bringing in its wake lessons of many kinds. I appreciate the direct way that Dr. Robert Svoboda says it: "Nature is conspiring to connect us to reality." Pandemic has appeared as Mother Nature's response to the accumulated choices of humanity, demanding that we reflect upon what is not in harmony, what is out of balance for us individually. The dominant culture of the world has spread like a virus to every corner of life on Earth, turning a blind eye to how we, as a species, are killing our planet in millions of acts of careless greed, injustice and violence.

As we teeter on the brink, there is much that is out of balance, but blaming others is not the solution. Each one of us is responsible to see how we are embedded in the belief of separation as soon as we are born and how that belief gives rise to the frantic, grasping activities of mind and emotion that fill up our inner space until we are suffocating.

If we're willing, we can get to the healing depths of ourselves, where we find that the broken heart has the power to sculpt a human being into a work of art. Our heartbreak can awaken us to a much bigger life, which may sound romantic or cliché, but in reality it's earthy and usually painful, occurring "in the trenches" and "on the streets" of our daily life circumstances and situations. No one is exempt. No matter how problem-free one's life may seem to be, sooner or later adversity will make cracks in our hearts. Will we have the inner strength to bear it? How can we give back to the world, when we have been blessed with so much? *Let yourself ponder what needs healing and restoration in your family, in your community, in your relationship to others and to the Earth.*

In the Emerald House

born from the soul of the world
where all things are connected
beyond time and place,
longing is sweet in moments
when I remember that
in loss there is gain, and
what is truly empty
becomes full again

this body is stardust
remembered from novas
and galaxies of light
strewn across black space,
trailing the ache of
a goddess at birth,

gaping and wide open,
a silent shout of joy

world mother, world sustainer
we are not shadows but your
incomprehensible children of union,
and though we were
never born and cannot die,
all this is real, every soul
is your delight, made by whim

why ponder such impossible things?
it is only my small attempt at praise,
bound and shattered here
in this emerald house of love

SEEING CLEARLY

We are molded and formed by the culture in which we are
embedded. Though we may have the idea that we are free, we live
in prisons so familiar that it's hard to see the bars of our small cell.
We have to recognize the traps of modern life—social, cultural,
religious, political—before we can be free to cultivate the strength
and clarity that we will need to meet whatever life brings to us.

"Know thyself," said Socrates and his student Plato, two of
the ancients of Western philosophy. For contemplation to make

a difference in the world, we must begin to see clearly, and this begins with ourselves. In the chapter ahead we return to this idea many times and in many ways. Putting down the defenses that block our own way, we can turn to the solutions of nonviolence and the awakened conscience. It's a journey that leads back again to the broken heart, but this is the key to finding the inner wholeness that comes from self-knowledge.

Be willing to grieve. In recent times I've heard others echo the depths of my own heart—there is a felt-sense of sadness about the plight of our planet and the horrific conditions of our world. The road of conscience is often a rocky way to go, but the grief that comes from bearing witness to the reality of *what is* carries a tremendous alchemical power within the crucible of the human heart.

At the time of this writing, early summer of 2020, protestors of racial inequity have been met by SWAT teams with clubs and tear gas. The tragedy of ever-present violence and abuse of power continues to escalate in the United States, catalyzing people to take to the streets with the outcry, "Black Lives Matter." When our contemplations help to carry this heavy load, compassion, generosity and kindness are cultivated in our hearts.

It hurts, yes. And we must allow ourselves to grieve, to feel the pain of it. Bringing awareness to global suffering is a powerful form of radical engagement with the world. It's an inner stance that cultivates an empathetic conscience that makes us truly human. As we hear the call of the inner life and turn toward the meeting with ourselves, we become aware that we are staging our own personal revolution on behalf of the world soul. Martin Prechtel has been speaking the voice of the indigenous people and their wisdom on grief, learned from hard experience:

> *Lastly, we've got to begin to grieve. Now, grief doesn't mean sitting around weeping every day. Rather, grief means using the gifts you've been given by the spirits to make beauty. Grief that's not expressed this way becomes a kind of toxic waste inside a person's body, and inside the culture as a whole, until it has to be put in containers and shipped someplace, the way they ship radioactive waste to New Mexico. This locked-up grief has to be metabolized. As a culture and as individuals, we must begin feeling our grief—that delicious, fantastic, eloquent medicine. Then we can start giving spiritual gifts to the land we live on, which might someday grant our grandchildren permission to live there.*

It starts with being honest about our own personal suffering, which sooner or later links us to the suffering of others. As we work to awaken and sustain our own awareness, we ask the essential questions: *Who am I? Where did I come from? Where am I going? What is my purpose here?* Making our questions more specific, we can contemplate more deeply, expanding and deepening our discernment: *Who am I in these powerful and terrible times? Where do I stand? What are the opportunities within this time of travail?*

Meister Eckhardt, the renowned theologian and Christian mystic, wrote centuries ago, "What we plant in the soil of contemplation, we shall reap in the harvest of action." We are called to the inner life because we are personally responsible for the fate of the world, and the situation becomes more urgent with each passing day. Contemplation connects to the deep intuition that can show us the way to go—how to move forward in action—while it ushers in a clear view of whatever blocks the door to true being.

> *The sorrow, grief, and rage you feel is a measure of your humanity and your evolutionary maturity. As your heart breaks open there will be room for the world to heal.*
>
> —Joanna Macy

THE ALCHEMY OF THE REAL

All life is suffering, as the Buddha said when he taught his first noble truth. In both Buddhism and Hinduism, this world is the realm of *dukkha*, the Sanskrit word that is translated as "suffering." We have an opportunity to see this deeply: the Earth suffers; her people, animals, plants, rivers and oceans and skies suffer. My teacher used to say, "Real suffering produces alchemical gold; ordinary suffering is just misery." I find this to be a rich source of inner questioning: What did he mean?

Going deeper with intention generates the heat and light of seeing clearly and feeling beneath superficial layers of ordinary suffering. Gathering up our courage, we take "a fearless moral inventory," as it's said in Twelve Step communities. It's important to ask questions that are empowering, that will ultimately move us toward an inner freedom. Here are some sample questions you might ask as a beginning inquiry. Take a few quiet moments now to consider one or more of these without needing to come up with concrete answers. Perhaps images or memories will show themselves to you, or sensations will arise. Note anything that really grabs your attention. Listen to the voice of your inner life. If you like, you can write down your reflections. Let these questions inspire others for you.

> *When and how do I avoid my own suffering?*
> *How do I shut out the pain of others?*
> *Am I willing to meet honestly with myself?*
> *What is truly necessary in my life?*

Referring to what he calls "necessary suffering," the contemporary Franciscan monk Father Richard Rohr wrote, "All great spirituality is about what we do with our pain. If we do not transform our pain, we will transmit it to those around us." The 18th-century poet John Keats called this "soul making." Contemplating our personal experience, we come to know the difference between the habitual, superficial suffering of our false sense of self and the authentic suffering of the deeper self. This essential discernment is how we begin to move from the trees to the forest, which takes us into a larger story or view that will alchemize the pain we feel.

Taking responsibility for the joys and sorrows of the soul is not a comfortable process. It's a stretching and opening and letting go that can be terrifying or merely painful. Ego will protest having its hidden motives (all about the survival of "me") revealed, and yet ego is necessary to being alive. We will never get rid of our egos! Nor would we want to. Ego is our window on the world, a kind of GPS for getting around. Ego can be harnessed to work cooperatively and even peacefully under the guidance of a higher or deeper boss—the self that includes the wisdom of experience and a well-developed conscience. When that happens, then we have a marvelous capacity to make good choices, to serve, and to act in positive ways.

We have to search within to discover the gold for ourselves, through our own experience, even though other wayfarers and guides can help point the way or affirm our experience. Before we move on for a deeper dive into contemplation, I'll explore two skills or attitudes, acceptance and simplicity, that can help us along the way.

Acceptance. The modern sage, Swami Prajnanpad, gave a simple reminding phrase for working with acceptance: "Not what should be but what is." Accepting whatever reality is bringing our way, here and now, is a powerful support that helps us maintain basic sanity and a grounded connection to life. As we move into deeper terrain of acceptance, the context of non-rejection becomes vital. If we cut away, try to destroy, stamp down, deny or repress what we fear, dislike or experience, sooner or later the very thing we've pushed away will show up, unexpectedly, in another way to cause problems.

At the same time that we embrace *what is* in a mood of acceptance, it's important to develop discernment and discipline.

We do not *act* on negative impulses but simply *see* them. Acceptance is not about condoning or acting upon life-negative impulses; it's a process of educating ourselves to see clearly and feel fully—our anger, for example—without acting upon it. Anger is full of vitality and energy and can help us gain clarity. Acting upon anger creates entanglements of negativity, causes suffering to others, and often backfires upon us. Instead of acting on angry impulse, we accept that it is present and seek to clarify and transform it into pure, powerful energy.

When acceptance is fully embodied and ensouled, it can bestow the precious gift of peace. Once, when I was twenty years old and wrestling with the turmoil that is particular to the very young, I asked my wonderful grandmother how she had so much peace in her life. She gave me one of those long, measuring looks and answered simply, "Acceptance. I accept everything."

Simplicity. Simplicity can be a blessed way to live that frees us from preoccupations and opens up the inner life. As we feel deeply into the dynamics of joy and sorrow, we begin to see how much suffering comes from our expectations, attachments and identifications. We begin to see that the desire for things—like the habits of being a consumer in a consumer society—is a form of suffering. The things we accumulate are not fulfilling our deeper needs.

Gaining clarity, we can slowly pare away attachments and identifications—both attractions and aversions—that are no longer necessary or useful for our spiritual growth. In that paring down, we discover what is essential to our well-being. Realizing that *less is more*, we can begin to voluntarily simplify our lives. To live more simply in a very complex world is no easy feat. It's a powerful and radical gesture toward healing ourselves and our world, where natural resources have been plundered, and in so many cases wasted, for centuries.

Moving toward simplicity and acceptance comes naturally when we are present with what is, as it is. These modes of being nurture what Swiss philosopher and psychiatrist Dr. Carl Jung called "the spacious personality." As we become more spacious within, we can let go of the burden of painful chronic tension and judgments. Our lives and relationships become more harmonious, more resilient and capable to meet life as it unfolds. Clearing and opening up a space within, we can listen deeply to follow the wise impulses of the soul, which lead us to discover a very natural unfolding of the simplicity that sets us free.

IV

Inner Yoga

Our consciousness always has the potential of finding its way back to wholeness, just as a child who has wandered away always has the possibility to rediscover and reunite with its mother.
—Lama Tsultrim Allione

The discipline of sahaja begins with the acceptance of the whole of life just as it is. The heart opens up to receive it and live it.
—Sri Anirvan

I believe life is a Zen koan, that is, an unsolvable riddle. But the contemplation of that riddle—even though it cannot be solved—is, in itself, transformative. And if the contemplation is of high enough quality, you can merge with the Divine.
—Tom Robbins

Yoga is anything we do that connects our humanity with our divinity. In hatha yoga, we stretch, strengthen, and release tension in the muscles and bones of the body as we hold and breathe through the posture. We become very intimate with where the muscles are weak, the breath is constricted or full, the joints are painful and bones are brittle. We work to develop the circulation of *prana* (life force), to expand and increase ease of movement, fluidity, radiant health and well-being. We get to know our bodies very well, and over time the outer yoga leads to an interior world.

The inner yoga of contemplation is similar, but it's centered in the world of you. And, while in some ways it's a science, it's most certainly an artform that yields a personal sacred space inside, where we live with ourselves.

In this chapter we'll inquire into some of the cornerstones upon which the inner temple is built, beginning with the study that leads to self-knowledge. With a very light touch, I'll weave in a few threads of the teachings that have been great inspirations for me, blended with my own synthesis and practical understanding of Jung's concepts of the inner life. As we travel down these particular inroads of contemplation, you will most likely encounter familiar concepts. Let them resound for you, as if you've stumbled upon an old friend, then see and feel into what comes welling up for you.

STUDY YOUR TRUE NATURE

When we study something, we pay close attention, observe and delve into it as a pathway to greater knowledge. Pursued over time, the self-study of contemplation awakens a creative intimacy with ourselves that will flower and bear fruit in myriad and surprising ways.

Study of all spiritual and religious traditions, as an intentional and heartfelt questing, continues to bear fruit for me, as I untangle and follow the threads of those deep matters that concern the journey of the soul through space and time and beyond. My passion for learning grew its first pair of wings when I read the Bhagavad Gita for the first time. I was nineteen years old then, but the inspired flame of study has burned steadily over the decades. Connecting the dots between my personal experience and the universal human experience, I've found that literature and art are also rich mines for contemplative study. Podcasts are fabulous resources, good for studying during walks and long drives. Films and documentaries are included in my practice of study because they arouse my curiosity and encourage me to ponder and reflect deeply. All this is fuel for contemplation.

During the Covid-19 pandemic, I followed my ardor for study into new territory, which led to a discovery of *lectio divina*, the practice of study that is found in the mystical Christian tradition. Reading a sacred text or inspirational book with a deep intention to connect with the Divine, we ask questions like, "How would I say this?" or "How is this occurring for me?" Rather than a heady, intellectual pursuit, study becomes grounded in personal insight. The soulful podcasts of James Finley, a contemporary Christian mystic and psychotherapist who lived and studied with Thomas Merton at the Abbey of Gethsemane, have opened new doors into Merton's teachings for me. But most of all, I've been deeply moved by Finley's direct experience of a loving God that is both mother and father.

It's been a revelation to access contemporary mystics emerging from the Roman Catholic Church. The courageous self-honesty and profound truth-telling I've found in the teachings and commentary of Father Richard Rohr, and his vision of the Universal Christ, has helped me to metabolize my anger and sorrow at the abuses of power heaped upon humanity by organized religions over centuries of time. As a person who grew up in the Methodist Church, then left it as a disillusioned adolescent, the teachings of these elders have helped me further release any lingering negative images of a wrathful God who created humans in original sin. In my opinion, reclaiming a universal spirituality that embraces original innocence and essential goodness is a great and necessary healing of the world soul.

THE UNIVERSAL VIEW

Sahaja is a yoga for the same reason as all other yogas.
It is a path that leads to the discovery of 'That with which
one is born,' the pure being living in the temple of the heart.
—Sri Anirvan

Eastern wisdom is like the Ganges, a river of many tributaries, where we can drink deeply of the teachings of the original goodness in human nature. Experiencing firsthand the vibrant spiritual cultures of India has been one of the greatest gifts of my personal journey. I'm grateful for those opportunities, especially being in the presence of the saint Yogi Ramsuratkumar, a person of rare, universal realization. Another important influence has been my association with the Bauls of Bengal—the mystic yogis, wandering singers, poets and revolutionaries of north India. I've been fortunate to know, befriend and travel with numerous Bauls, to learn a few of their songs and imbibe their earthy mysticism.

The Bauls are champions of the evolutionary potential of human beings. For the past five hundred years, they have renounced their caste status and religious creeds, dogmas and doctrines of all kinds to delve into a personal search for the illusive beloved of the heart and their innate true nature, which they call *sahaja*. I like to use this Sanskrit word because it means "easy, natural, spontaneous and primordial."

My teacher used the term "organic innocence" to describe the true nature of human beings. Similarly, Tibetan Buddhist teachings have given us the useful phrase "basic goodness." Both of these expressions dovetail with the natural movements of *sahaja* celebrated by the Bauls. Many traditions teach that the ground of the self is intrinsically good. But again, we have to investigate and affirm this truth for ourselves.

Let's ponder the word "goodness" for a moment, seeking its depths. The much-used word "good" comes from Old English with even older Germanic roots in the word *ghedh*, which means "to gather or bring together"—another way of saying "to unify." This is a very good (no pun intended) description of the evolutionary force of the self moving toward an inclusive wholeness and unity that interpenetrates both inner and outer, including everyone and everything. It's a mystical fusion of unity (the nondual) and diversity, or the dual nature of the reality in which we live and breathe.

Innate sahaja knows and feels and expresses the connectivity it shares with flowers, trees, bumblebees, lions, rattlesnakes and butterflies, with disasters like fires and floods and earthquakes, with all human beings everywhere, even with riots and SWAT teams and tear gas, with newborn babies and hungry people, with the planets of our solar system, with stars and galaxies and black holes. And in this way, sahaja resonates with "the greening of the self"—a term from the work of scholar and environmentalist Joanna Macy, who blends the Buddhist teaching that there is no separate self with the emerging idea of an ecological self that is co-arising and co-dependent with all of life. It's a view that cuts through dualistic concepts and places a supreme emphasis on the web of life as co-emergent, alive and interdependent. It's a profound view worth investigating.

As an ardent theist and pantheist, I often return to the Baul perspective because it spans the seeming chasm between unity (or nondualism) and the diversity of existence. For the Bauls, *sahaja* is a spontaneous dance or marriage between nonduality and duality that exists in the play of the moment. Arising from the ground of being, sahaja carries intuitive wisdom that, allowed to move our lives, frees us from inner struggle or agonizing over decisions. Connected to the source within, what direction or decision to take becomes tacit and obvious. As Sri Anirvan wrote, "There is no greater yoga than to be perfectly natural."

Baul teachings on sahaja have a beautiful simplicity that rests upon the elegant foundations of the vast, ancient wisdom traditions of India. For example, one of India's most prominent schools of philosophy, Vedanta, teaches that the deep self of the individual is called *atman*, which has its existence in the universal or supreme self, or *paramatman*—a microcosm of the macrocosm.

Built upon the terra firma of self-knowledge, the art of contemplation flourishes to bear the sweetest fruit, as well as the most viable seeds. The *bhakti* (devotional) traditions are rooted in the Bhagavad Gita, wherein the Lord Krishna gives his teachings on yoga beginning with the yoga of integral awareness and knowledge, or *buddhi* (from the root word *budh*, meaning to wake up or discern). On the path to liberation, this is the foundation yoga that the essential nature of the soul, or *svabhava*, engages. The Sanskrit word *sva* is often translated as self and *bhava* is a word that refers to mood or felt tones that resonate—which gives an important hint that the self or soul has not only awareness but also qualities of deep feeling. The benefits of studying many different ways of viewing the self or true nature are countless across all boundaries of religion or psychology.

A SCHOLAR OF THE SELF

The primordial goodness of sahaja and svabhava is ever-present within us, but we still have to gain access to it in a process of uncovering, recovering and discovering the self. It's about becoming a scholar—a learned person—of our own self.

In the twentieth century, the terms "self" and "shadow" were posed for the West by the brilliant visionary, C.G. Jung, whose work infused the field of transpersonal psychology. Both psychiatrist and philosopher, Jung was a scientist who immersed himself in Eastern and Western spiritual traditions. Jung's wisdom gives form to a practical template for working with what often seems chaotic, scary or just plain confusing in our experience of life. His work is a necessary bridge over the divide between spirituality and psychology and has been a great help to me personally in my ongoing process of inner yoga. Although widespread in usage within our contemporary culture, I'll explore my own synthesis and perspective of Jung's notions of self and shadow.

Dr. Jung referred to the self as "the archetype of wholeness," often using the symbolic image of a mandala—pairs of opposites that exist within a unifying circle of oneness—to convey the nondual and dual aspects of the self. The mandala of the self is an organizing principle within human beings that exists beneath the superficial aspects of our human experience. Underlying our familiar personalities, which Jung called the "persona," is the primordial power of the deep self. Rather than static or perfect, the self is a flow of diversity that moves toward oneness. The self is transpersonal, mediating boundaries between what is known and unknown, between human and divine. As the late psychologist, Marion Woodman, put it in her book, *The Maiden King*:

> *We are both animal and divine. In our essence, the opposites are not in opposition. In an electromagnetic field, same poles of a magnet repel each other, opposite poles attract, creating a tension that is attempting to pull them together. If we can hold at the center of the tension, our hearts will open, will be opened, by love greater than we have ever known.*

REFLECTING ON THE OPPOSITES

With our attention placed in the inner world, we begin to see that we are moving back and forth between two shores or a pair of opposites, usually in reaction against one or both.

One of Jung's great insights is the transforming alchemical power of holding the tension of the opposites that are at play within us. When we stand firmly on the bridge between opposing forces inside ourselves (or in the tension between our inner reaction to an outer circumstance), a reconciling power may arise. Holding an inclusive perspective of acceptance in the betwixt and between of Celtic lore, magic can happen. When that occurs, sometimes we catch a glimpse of what is beyond the opposites.

Sometimes the opposites are obvious: we rebound between fear and courage, between yes and no. We feel love and hate, maybe even so close together that they seem present at the same time.

We're happy for our friend, but we're also jealous. We feel terribly sad, and yet joy bubbles up in the cracks. We want to forgive, but we nurse our resentment with fervor!

This tension between the opposites may take some time to resolve when we feel paralyzed. When my teacher died, I'd lived for twenty years in the all-encompassing warmth of an intimate relationship with him that required I give up everything—career, independence and identity. The spiritual path opened up for me in many ways as I lived and traveled around the world with Lee, at home in the warmth and graceful flow of his company. When he died at age sixty-six of cancer, everything changed for me. Raw grief and shock held me in its grip. Life as I had known it fell apart in an ongoing series of disintegrations that, at age sixty, took me to the threshold of my psychological and spiritual endurance. Sheltered for so long in his company, living anonymously "in the shadow of greatness" as the saying goes, I struggled with painful uncertainty and hesitation, while a fiery urgency called me to begin anew in the open space of possibilities.

As I wrestled with these opposites, I continued to live on the ashram in between travels. At some point, invitations to give workshops and public talks, to sing *bhajans* with friends on the path, called me out of seclusion and conspired to usher me further down the road of life. The wonderful event of falling in love with an old friend who is now my husband, Thomas, brought full-on magic into my life, and with it, a natural renewal of the soul.

In the play of the opposites, unless we bring them to our awareness, we can wither away in a fog of indecision for years.

When the stakes are high and any move we make will most certainly cause big changes and loss for ourselves and others, then it becomes extremely difficult to get clarity and act. Of course, having sensitivity to timing is important. Sometimes we need to wait and weigh the factors, allowing ourselves time and space to contemplate the opposing sides of a situation.

How can we know whether to act or to wait? We do the necessary work to gain clarity, remembering that we're not looking for resolution or to fix things. To alchemize a situation that is inner or outer, we need to be present with what is and be aware of the play in the tension between the two poles. From that middle ground, creative unknowns and reconciling wisdom may arise, or pure grace intervenes, even when the decisive move, when it comes, may ultimately be irrevocable.

Whether we call it grace or serendipity, something occurs in the heat and friction of the in-between, the middle place that moves the situation forward. In contemplation, we can cultivate an ability to be suspended *in reflection*, to dive into introspection and hold the tension between opposing forces until insight arrives from within our own depths or in an unexpected outer event. Inevitably, our inner quest will lead to a breakthrough.

THE PROCESS OF INDIVIDUATION

We are always beginners in the process of linking the ordinary self, which functions on the surface of life, with the deepest self. The self is a mystery that keeps revealing itself, moving beyond gender, beyond conflict, beyond oppositions. This gift of an expanding, maturing, integrated awareness is what Jung called "the process of individuation." American Buddhist teacher Lama Tsultrim Allione speaks eloquently of this process, which leads to a greater sense of being interconnected with all of life: "Our mandala interfaces with others' mandalas. It becomes a beautiful, pulsating mandala, a matrix of overlaid mandalas. When seen this way, our lives are an intricate interwoven fabric."

The individuation journey is one of bringing into consciousness that which is unconscious and integrating the joys and sorrows of a life well-lived. Instead of denial or avoidance as a way of life, we bring aspects of who we are into awareness so that we can see, clarify and integrate those into the mandala—the wholeness vision—of our individuality. When we live fully and digest our experience in a process of integration at all levels of our being, every time we meet and move through a challenge or difficulty in life, it lives within us as wisdom.

Being schooled by my own experience, I've found that there are many interwoven threads of continuity between the levels of my awareness—between the deepest self and the surface self. These different levels or aspects of "me" are interdependent and reciprocal, like everything else in life. A central theme of self-study is how the attitudes and beliefs we hold on the surface can block or open the connection with the deep self. One powerful example of this is the cultural and religious belief that encourages a fear of emptiness. While the surface self of personality may avoid the depths with the buffers of addictions and compulsions, the deep self is at home with the sense of inner emptiness, while it just as easily dances with the ten thousand things of an active life.

Jung's term "the shadow" is connected to the natural experience of emptiness because it refers to the mystery of everything that is unknown to the conscious mind. As the inner yoga of contemplation grows, we begin to realize that we cannot know the self without knowing its shadow, or unknown dimensions of self. That means we have to take a deeper dive into the mystery, called by the lure of what glimmers there.

HIDDEN GOLD

Cultural and religious biases make it easy to fall into the idea that the shadow is something sinful or bad in a moral sense—a view that has resulted in terrible misunderstandings and great suffering on planet Earth. We may have to work very hard to re-envision a concept of the shadow as unlived creative potentials that are inherent in the blueprint of our own true nature. These potentials are sometimes referred to as the "bright shadow," which carries with it the greatness of our hidden gifts and talents. As we follow this way, it's important to find a balanced intermingling of the *via positiva* and the *via negativa*, to borrow terms from ancient philosophers, found echoed in the contemporary work of Matthew Fox.

As we reframe our view of the "negative" aspects of ourselves, we can begin to see that, just as Jung discovered, the shadow is shaped by wounds and traumas, or by natural dimensions of life—

like sex and death—that are repressed and denied. The shadow has autonomy, so that it acts from its place in the unconscious, sometimes in ways that surprise or alarm. Like a pot boiling over, denied long enough, haunted by wounds and terrors of many kinds, the shadow can be split off from its deep source of goodness, becoming pathological as it seeks to express its evolutionary (and revolutionary) impulse toward the self.

These two—self and shadow—often function as a pair of opposites with unbearable tension between them. I experience them as a continuum that has its source in the primordial depths of sahaja. The shadow contains and manifests the ways that we are stuck and grinding away at the obstacles and very real traumatic experiences lodged within our own complicated experience of who we believe we are. But, as dark as it may seem, the shadow also contains and manifests the inner urge of the self toward our uniquely individual potentials.

As Jung pointed out, working with the shadow requires moral courage, spiritual fortitude and a deep desire for truth or reality. Working with the shadow is a healing process when we give ourselves permission to be friendly and curious along the way, rather than falling into a default of blame, guilt, shame or cynicism. Tremendous energy is bound up in the shadow and its complexes that live at the core of our wounds. Unraveling the knots and untangling the threads creates inner space, and gives some breathing room and glimpses of freedom along the way.

This may be a good time to stop and reflect: *Do you recognize your true nature when it whispers to you? Do you rest in knowing that your essential nature is good? Are you swayed by the superficial? Have you taken the time to contemplate the woundings and traumas you've endured, or to be honest about the empty feeling beneath your addictions and compulsions? Let these questions be a part of your contemplative moments.*

Whether our interior work is easy or hard—and it will be some of both—it's a process catalyzed by the template for wholeness in the deep self. Super-charged with the energy and power of the primordial life force, integrating shadow material can shake us to the core of our foundations.

For example, we receive a shock in the form of an event that occurs, or someone says something that is true but disturbing. The false views or illusions we harbor can be dismantled in many different ways by the movements of life. We can learn to make use of these natural impulses toward growth and transformation that sometimes intrude into our conscious awareness exactly when we least expect it. As terrifying or upsetting or hard to bear as these interventions of the self may be in moments, they are essential to our evolution and ultimate freedom.

One way to begin or continue to learn about ourselves is to start with "the outer" and progress to "the inner." By studying the body and using our five senses, we get to see how the shadow shows up during our interactions or when we are alone. Seeing impartially, we can observe many things about ourselves—like how we breathe. It's always fruitful to pay attention to our breath, to notice how we hold it, and to be aware of our breathing patterns. Even thinking about a stressful situation when we're alone and relaxed can change our breathing pattern until we are literally holding our breath.

Learning from observation, the body offers many clues—like how we squirm or fidget or turn away when we hear something we don't like. Or how we sit or stand with arms crossed over chest or a hand clamped over the mouth when we feel threatened. How we stop breathing when we're anxious or scared. The power of perceptive seeing and witnessing begins "at home," but of course we can gain a great deal of insight into how this all works by observing the behaviors of others. It's almost always easier to see the shadow in someone else!

This is tricky territory, because we really do not know what is going on with another person underneath the surface, and it's easy to be fiercely judgmental. But we can train ourselves to let go of the superiority of judgment and apply what we've observed in others to ourselves, knowing that what we are seeing "out there" is also, in some way, a mirror of what is "in here." An honest process of self-observation cultivates very deep compassion for ourselves and others.

Judgment, being superior, thinking we know better, dominating, controlling, passive aggression, narcissism and the failure to bring empathy to others…we're really good at our own shadow play because we learned to survive this way from an early age. Our underground defense systems are deep-rooted in the real need to maintain a safety net or buffer. Now that we are becoming more compassionate and resilient in working with reality as it is, we may discover that we have the courage of our conviction, which builds many virtues. We can start to tear down our walls and put down our weapons of defense. Over time and with diligence, we are building strength, clarity, confidence and compassion.

As we go deeper into our own minds and emotions to see what's going on there, we can ask questions that empower and clarify our relationship with ourselves: *What aspects of myself (and others) do I avoid? How and when am I selfish? What moods do I experience and express a lot of the time?* Sadness…anger…frustration…jealousy… fear…hatred…the drive to be right, to have power? What about disappointment…joy…gratitude…pain…bliss…disgust… terror…love…cynicism or sorrow?

Embracing self and shadow, we come to know ourselves in a continuous awareness of all our aspects—beautiful and ugly, dark and light, good and bad. A contemplative relationship with ourselves built over time can help us overcome chronic insecurity and confusion to gain the confidence and compassion necessary to work with the tidal pull of emotions. Learning to see and feel the inner currents, then let them go in the moment, we become more resilient, flexible and spacious. It's the magic of *letting go* that is transformative.

V

Obstacles and Opportunities

*Although most of modern life is arranged to take us away from
ourselves, the soul is always on the verge of some great awareness
and on the edge of awakening to a more genuine way of being.*
—Michael Meade

*Developing a more spacious personality, to use Jung's felicitous phrase,
sounds pleasant, but seldom do we grow toward one without the
old order being called into account. It is generally through the
experience of unsolicited suffering that we grow larger,
not because the unexamined life proved easier.*
—James Hollis

When we make the inner quest, inevitably we will discover that there are obstacles in the way. And yet, obstacles can reveal the virtue and life-giving nourishment beneath the confusing turmoil of an emotionally charged situation or inner conflict. To deal with inevitable roadblocks, we need a new attitude, a new approach that helps us to see the opportunities within the obstacles.

Maybe we feel that we've already done this work. We've been on the path for many years. We might have practiced inquiry in some form, like asking "Who am I?" Or, we've been through psychotherapy. Everything we've done is a useful part of us, and yet, the question remains—who am I *now*? The point is, keep going. Stay with it. We are a great mystery to ourselves, a mystery that is being revealed in an ongoing, looping spiral within the ever-changing mandala of the self. We can catch glimpses of that mystery every day, even in ordinary circumstances, when we continue to inquire, looking for the opportunities hidden within the obstacles.

COMPLEXITY AND CHAOS

The first obstacle we encounter is the pace and demand of modern life, where we juggle stress, complexity and chaos on a daily basis. Life in the world as it is today does not offer much, if any, support to be introspective or to develop the contemplative side of ourselves. Even the thought of "going within" to explore an interior wilderness, or of "inner stillness" and "receptive emptiness," is often met with serious resistance from ourselves or others.

One way to break through obstacles is by learning how to inquire within. Ask yourself questions that open the doors of contemplation. When we are overwhelmed by the complexity of daily life—and our own complicated inner labyrinth—it's good to keep it really simple: *What do I see and feel? What do I love? What do I fear? What do I really want? What stands in the way?*

Although you will certainly ask them, you may find that questions beginning with "why" are a dead-end street. Maybe that's because "why" is already tinged with presuppositions of fear and judgment. Questions that ask "why" tend to seek out concrete answers that lead to closed doors. In my experience, those questions that begin with *how, when, where, who* and *in what way* are more open-ended and fruitful. If you like to write, trying jotting down your reflections or exploring them with wordplay. Perhaps you'd prefer to take a walk with one of the following questions in mind. Or, simply pose them to yourself as you enter into stillness.

What brightens or darkens my mood?
When do I have a feeling or awareness of flow?
Where and when am I spontaneous, natural?
How and in what way do I have clarity?
How am I when physical or emotional pain is present for me?
When do I feel confused, stressed out, self-conscious, miserable?

What brings me joy, what brings me sorrow?
Am I able to live with and be enriched by both?

We're not looking for answers engraved on a stone tablet. We're not seeking formulas or scriptures that might relieve us of the pain of personal responsibility. We're looking for insight and self-knowledge. Be keenly interested in simplicity and the liberating power of awareness that moves you in a more positive direction, for yourself, for others and for the world. Court the possibility of revelation and wonder by getting to know your own obstacles.

CYNICISM & SPEED

Everyday life serves up a rich table of dishes, each one a feast for the metabolism of our digestion process. Take cynicism, for example. It's something I can write about because I know it so well in myself. Rampant in our world today, cynicism is a common defensive response to the troubled emotions that we feel and the traumas we have endured. Hiding behind many of our attitudes toward life, cynicism defends us from being shattered by our own grief about the suffering in the world.

Cynicism is different from pragmatic realism or from the "street wisdom" that cuts through what is unreal and illusory. Rather than acutely perceptive, cynicism is often sarcastic or droll. Cynicism can lead to indifference, apathy and passive aggression. Allowed to take over, cynicism accumulates in a deadening of the soul, while we're busy running some type of marathon in an achievement-driven culture. Busy, busy, busy, we don't even notice that the soul is begging for us to just let go and do nothing. It's often a cover-up for despair and desperation, two common emotions we will return to in the next chapter.

Our cool and sophisticated cynicism is self-protective and serves a purpose in the psyche, so until we have developed a capacity to live in reality as it is, it may need to stay in place. We can become aware of our cynicism, observe it, watch it like a movie with a friendly and curious attitude. But, let's not forget that while our cynical attitudes and fast-paced repartees are effective at buffering us against a painful world, they are also smokescreens for anger and despair. Most of all, they block the way to innate, divine qualities like innocence, joy, awe and wonder.

As for speed, our Western culture places a high demand and premium on speed and drive that create obstacles of stress and even anger. We drive ourselves into high speed for apparently good reasons that are, at the same time, entangled with ideals of perfectionism, accomplishment, acknowledgement and personal achievement. When we're in overdrive to get things done, anger can accumulate until we flare up in a moment of rage. We're just not open to hearing the message from within that's saying, please, slow down and take some time to be quiet, silent, still...

Here's another theme that is quite familiar to me. I love to plan and get things done, especially when it comes to creative projects like writing. I know from experience that speed and drive can be self-centered and out of relationship with others. When I've taken on too much and there's no end in sight, stress-related anger creeps in. When that's happening, I'm out of touch with myself. Obsessions are often fueled by the super-charge of anger, which sooner or later take a huge toll on the health of our own bodies, not to mention on the joy, love and spontaneity in relationships.

Having done this myself, I can say from experience that when we finally realize that we are worn down and suffering from exhaustion, strained relationships, and possibly faced with life-changing health issues, the only way to restore balance and health is to go within. Following the trail from complexity to simplicity, we can bring sanity to our inner and outer world. All obstacles respond in a positive way when we rest in what is essential in life.

Is there a connection between your own fast drive and an underlying cynical mindset? In your speed, do you leave behind a trail of "broken and bleeding bodies," including your own? Are you cynical about the price you're paying for all of that?

HERE WE GO AGAIN

We've all noticed that life occurs in cycles and things repeat themselves. Returning to an event, a memory, a conversation, or replaying the past in an unconscious hope to get some resolve are the fare of daily life commonly shared by all. As the psyche seeks to integrate difficult aspects of life that are hard to bear, rumination and recapitulation can be useful aspects of contemplation—if we're aware that we are replaying the past because there is something there that we still need to work with.

When we are dwelling upon something, the key is to know how and what is actually useful—and for how long. Self-obsession can lead down a rabbit hole to a dead end, while a true process of integration will inevitably lead to bigger perspectives, flexibility, a sense of rebirth and greater freedom. When we're driving our contemplative vehicle down the road of repetitive rumination and recapitulation, we can learn a lot by wondering whether the direction we're headed in leads to a roadblock or an open field.

Rumination. Rumination goes over and over the same thoughts in a circular loop. This can be a positive process of digestion—in fact, the definition of rumination says that it also means repeatedly chewing. It's useful to contemplation until it becomes an obsessive pattern, like when worry leads to anxiety that escalates into panic.

A helpful yardstick is that obsession and obsessive behavior always express the shadow side of the self. When we're like a wheel spinning in a muddy rut, then we need to take a penetrating and courageous look at what's going on. Maybe we need to let go of a situation or relationship. Maybe we need to let go of ideas and concepts. For example, a commitment to being a surrendered devotee, a perfect yogi, or the best disciple—be it Hindu, Buddhist, Christian or any other—can be creative, propelling us into vast vistas, or it can become a dead end of festering guilt and shame that is detrimental to our well-being.

When emotions run hot and at high tide, we have no inner space to contemplate what the soul is really calling for. When we find ourselves in a situation of recurring obsessive rumination, and we are convinced that we are trapped with no way out, we face another all-too-familiar obstacle. Yet, here is a simple truth: *There is always a way out.* We just don't like our options, because they require or demand for us to let go, to make a sacrifice, or to surrender to some kind of death of what has been. They demand a confrontation with the unknown. They require a leap of faith.

Recapitulation. To recapitulate is to "summarize and repeat the main points of a case or argument," and also "to repeat the principle stages of a process." Recapitulation is close kin to rumination, which is useful to the process of digesting and integrating the nutrients that we consume every day at all levels in life. Yet, we need to ask ourselves, *how much time do we need to spend in rumination, or how many times do we need to recapitulate something?*

It's a natural part of growing older to look back over life, seeing and perceiving more as we replay past events and experiences. In the process we uncover deeper meaning, move toward a bigger picture. This process usually involves the kind of insight that gives a new context for a major life event. On the creative side of recapitulation is a spiraling process of return that is natural.

The symbol of the spiral appears everywhere in nature— nautilus shells, ferns, galaxies and flowers. It's one of the most common motifs found in the rock art of indigenous people around the world. I've found it in petroglyphs, painstakingly carved or pecked into rock walls throughout the Southwest, and in the five-thousand-year-old tumulus burial mounds of Bretagne, France.

Spirals are linked to the "thin places" of the Celts and the ancient ones who built the standing stones of Europe. The spectacular, 5200-year-old Stone-Age Newgrange passage tomb in Ireland has large spirals carved into its entrance. These are just a few examples of how prolific this symbol is in the ancient world.

As we recapitulate powerful archetypal experiences, especially those epic, almost mythological experiences that have changed our lives, we can recognize the patterns of our own spiral process. Seeing the spiral at work in our own lives can help us to let go and trust that whatever is necessary will come back later if we still need to work with it. When depth experiences are constellated around strong core feelings—like fear, grief, sorrow, betrayal or remorse—and relentlessly continue to arise for my recapitulation and rumination, they have something to tell me. They are trying to get my attention so that I can dig myself out of a rut of some kind. They are saying, "Time to go deeper, move, explore, let go…"

Wisdom has a delicate sense of timing. The ancient Greeks had a concept of *kairos*—that mysterious moment when all the cosmos, the planets in the solar system, and every vector of the subtle world lines up to the right time for action, both inner and outer. When we effectively recapitulate something in our lives, the experience ripens within us. When the time is right, we will need to let go and move on. The soul has its own timing in this, and as we cultivate contemplation, we can begin to hear the quiet inner voice that tells us when it's time.

TRUST THE WANDERER

One of the great, healing opportunities of contemplation is that there are no rules, no techniques or formulas. We are wanderers in the inner world, following a stream of consciousness that needs to flow freely. We can let go of concepts, including the concepts of rumination and recapitulation that we've just explored! As we build clarity and the strong intention to benefit ourselves and all of life, we can trust our contemplative roaming, guided by an inner compass.

You may be wondering if there is a place in contemplation for mantras, counting breaths or other yogic techniques. I was trained in many of these and continue to find them tremendously beneficial. Contemplation does not replace meditation, mantra, hatha yoga or any other specific spiritual discipline. In my experience, they each have a unique and vital place in the soul's journey. Contemplation is a mood or context that runs through all of these practices.

If you have a mantra or breath practice, it's likely these will come up in moments of contemplation. That's great! It's actually a sign that our mantra practice is taking root in us. When a mantra comes up naturally and easily, it has the flavor of grace or a divine inspiration. When mantras or breath practices arise naturally and spontaneously in this way, go with them and relish the moment. If they become a forced march or willful effort (again, there is absolutely a place and time for that kind of disciplined practice), then gently let go and pick up the thread of contemplation's spontaneous simplicity.

In contemplation we learn to trust our innate wisdom. Allow yourself to be a wayfarer, an explorer of the unknown. Set your intention and aim toward the greatest good for all (which includes you) and give in to the mystery. Trust in the benevolence and mercy of the Divine, the Universe, Life…and let go. The mood of trust is the ground that courage stands upon. It's far more profound as an ally than we can imagine. Trust is very, very close to faith and far, far away from mere belief.

VI

The Contemplative Descent

When it is dark, you can see the stars.
—Persian Proverb

So you must not be frightened if a sadness rises up before you,
larger than any you have ever seen; if a restiveness, like light
and cloud shadows, passes over your hands and over all you do.
You must think that something is happening with you, that life
has not forgotten you, that it holds you in its hand; it will not
let you fall. Why do you want to shut out of your life any uneasiness,
any miseries, or any depressions? For after all, you do not know
what work these conditions are doing inside you.
—Rainer Maria Rilke
Letters to a Young Poet

There are times when life gives us no choice but to go to a deeper place within, where we are forced to dwell upon our experience in ways that we may find disturbing or even frightening. Even if there was no pandemic or climate change, life would inevitably seize or thrust us into "D-times" of depression, dislocation, disillusionment, doubt, despair, deconstruction, dis-ease. The times of inner descent will certainly provide opportunities to make alliances with other strong emotions and feelings like anger and grief, two familiar and powerful players of the inner world.

These are universal human experiences that dissolve and deconstruct us, when our usual reality becomes unstable and we are left groundless, bereft and inconsolable. When we feel groundless, we usually hold on for dear life. We don't yet know that letting go will lead us, eventually, to feel at home in a wildly creative, evolving Universe.

When the D-times arrive, all of our comfortable reference points no longer have the power to keep us in control. As Saint John of the Cross described in his famous book, *Dark Night of the Soul*, it may seem that faith has flown away and cowers somewhere in a dark cave while we look into a dry ghost land of formless fear and anxiety. Sometimes depression and doubt arrive for no reason at all, for these very human experiences are not rational but mysterious. Whether we are dragged down into the depths because of outer events or inner mysteries, these experiences are a part of our humanity expressed in stories and myths from around the world, which mythology refers to as "the descent to the underworld."

> *"The Descent" is a mythological term for the period during and after a powerful event in which the ego has been overwhelmed by a wave from the unconscious. This is known as journeying into the underworld, a state in which creative energies are going through transformations that the unaware ego may know nothing about until big changes begin to happen in the outer world, or the studio begins to shine with totally new pictures, new music, or new sculpture. New images grow in the darkness of the creative mother. The goal of the descent is a new connection between earth and spirit.*
> —Marion Woodman

Living fully and honestly through times of great uncertainty and angst, and being willing to feel deeply, we can realize that it's not just about meaningless misery—it's an arc of experience that has purpose and potential. If we've avoided ourselves for a few years or a few decades, we can take heart knowing that we are in a process that spirals through experience that is digested and metabolized at different levels over time.

ALLIES IN THE FEARSOME PLACES

The truth is that without the D's many if not most of us would avoid those reflective moments that meander into dark, overgrown jungles or float downstream toward dangerous whitewater rapids and scary falls. We can find many reasons why we avoid a straightforward, honest relationship with these parts of ourselves. Of course, the ten-thousand things of life have a way of multiplying and keeping us busy. But as we peel away the layers of reasonable caution, for most of us it comes down to one simple truth—we are afraid. We fear the unknown, and fear makes our blood run cold.

Fear doesn't visit once and then go away because we've faced it. In my experience, fear comes back again and again. Fear is a natural response that can become a chronic, painful psychological state. We may try to argue and bargain with fear, or we scold ourselves. "I'm a courageous person. I do not feel fear." Or, "I'm an adult, I should be beyond childish fears." It's true that we're adults, but it doesn't matter how old we are—we're still in a process of growing up and into wisdom. At whatever age we begin or return again to renew the work of getting to know ourselves, there's always more to do. It's a lifetime process. As Dr. Jung noted, for most (but not all) of us, it doesn't even begin until we're over forty.

Even though the D's can be terrifying and crippling, that doesn't mean we should reject them. Fear in its many forms is telling us something we need to know. Actually, fear needs us to accept and feel it, to learn from its alarm bells. Bring fear to the table, give fear some attention and care, just as we would a guest. Pay attention to fear. Depression, which usually has some repressed anger beneath its surface, is often accompanied by another expression of fear: anxiety. These descent experiences all need a place at the table, as does the emotional shutdown of despair, disillusionment, apathy and indifference. Being disheartened, apathetic or anxious are powerful emotions that can paralyze us, striking at the heart of our faith in life, in God, in humanity.

As we learn that fearsome fear has something to show and teach, we become able to access the personal wisdom to act appropriately in the face of fear, which is true fearlessness. Maybe the opposite of love is not hate, as we often think, but fear. In my experience, hate has a place in the continuum of the vast, complex experience of love. Verify for yourself what the sages tell us: Love is the only real cure for fear and all maladies of the soul. Love is all-inclusive. Love embraces all and because of that, love is very close to trust.

Anxiety. The World Health Organization tells us that, by the year 2032, the world's number one health concerns will be depression and anxiety. Fear's potent child, anxiety, often comes hand-in-hand with depression and many of the other D's. Facing it in an honest way is tremendously empowering, for anxiety often comes with heavy doses of feeling powerless.

Anxiety runs very high for many people. Working with your breath is one of the most effective ways to calm anxious states that cause shortness of breath and emotional panic. Breathing evenly through your nose and focusing on the out breath, which is a physical letting go, can be very helpful when you feel anxious. For more information on the vital healing power of breath, I've found James Nestor's groundbreaking book, titled *Breath*, to be an excellent resource.

Fear and anxiety rumble beneath the surface of apathy. Fueled by raw fear, anxiety is a strong emotional force that grips us and shakes us hard until we are stunned senseless, leaving its mark of misery in listlessness and indifference. It's hard to know what to do in the moment when we cannot reason, trust or relax our way out of the strangle-hold of an emotion. If we can remember to use our capacity for acceptance, we can begin to help ourselves while we're battling the underworld beast.

I'm not expecting the D's to disappear. I'm no longer hoping to heroically banish depression or anxiety forever, like St. Michael killing the pagan dragon. What interests me is how to harness the power of these mind and body states for self-knowledge and transformation. Just imagine what would've happened if, instead of killing the great, beautiful, iridescent beast, the archangel Michael (despite the wild beating of his terrified heart) climbed on its back and took flight?

Affirm what is true. Honoring our feelings and emotions not only creates space but also opens up sources of energy so that we are not paralyzed but can act, even in the face of fear or despair. When besieged by one of the D's, I ask myself the question: "What is real here and now?" It's profoundly freeing when we tell the truth to ourselves about how and what we are feeling. In the act of doing so, we empower ourselves and simultaneously grant the possibility that there could be something sacred and mysterious afoot, even in this, our depression, angst and misery. Bringing attention and presence to an emotional state in this way can be a liberating form of contemplation that can return us to the underlying unity of the present moment.

As a writer, over the years I've taken the sage advice from Ernest Hemingway, who won the Nobel Prize for literature in 1954: "All you have to do is write one true sentence. Write the truest sentence you know." I always share this wisdom in my writing workshops because experience has taught me the efficacy and truth of it. It fits beautifully with the words of my spiritual teacher, Lee, who recommended the statement "This is real" to assert reality as it is. When I say, "This is real," I affirm my experience and let it be what it is. This simple, helpful practice is a way of having courage in the face of fear, which is really what fearlessness is about. Try looking any and all of the D's full on in the face and naming them. "This is depression. What I feel right now is fear. This is anxiety. I am here."

When Covid-19 first hit the States full on back in early March 2020, it took about six weeks for my old friend depression to arrive for an extended visit. I found myself face-to-face with the situation in the world today and heartbroken over events occurring in the U.S. while, simultaneously, I had to cancel a trip with my husband to Europe, where we had planned to visit his family and many long-time friends. I would have been giving several workshops while there as well. Isolated from friends and family, sheltering in place with Thomas (for whom I am eternally grateful), facing the coming realities of life on Earth and wrestling with chronic pain on the personal level, I floundered about in the murk until I woke up one morning and said out loud, "This is depression." As the weeks and months progressed, I began to realize that I needed to grieve. I needed to mourn the passing of the world as I've known it so that I could begin to make some space inside for what is now.

Renaissance

> After a long dark
> night of struggle
> one drop of
> distilled joy,
> elixir of mercy,
> causes this heart
> to open and
> tremble

Dreams. Dreams can be an excellent source of help, offered from within our own depths, and will often be particularly strong during descent times. Dream images can help us get down to the truth about emotional states. Working with dreams is an ancient, well-known form of inner yoga. One simple way to work with dreams is simply to contemplate the images. Ponder them without trying to analyze or intellectually understand them. Just allow them to resonate in your body and see what comes naturally. In this regard, I've appreciated the advice of Jungian scholar and psychologist, the late James Hillman, whose many writings and books are easy to find.

Some poets (like Dante, who wrote *The Inferno* about his famous descent into hell) say that the netherworld not only burns but also has an icy-cold dimension. I have found this to be true for myself, clients and friends who have shared their dreams over the years. Dreams will often reflect when someone is in the D-times with images of frozen lakes, snowy landscapes and icy water. These reflect our paralysis, the frozen wasteland inside, and are reminding us that inner work is needed to melt the ice back into its original state, so that genuine feeling is free to flow. At times when we are inundated by emotional states or deeper feelings, dream images of water come as tidal waves and floods, telling us that we are overwhelmed. Whatever the water is like, dreams carry important messages and wisdom; they can help us allow and honor our true feelings.

Wish-fulfilling Gems. Contemplation is a wish-fulfilling gem of many facets. When the terrible D's are what life has given us to work with—and maybe as a chronic, debilitating mood that persists for a long time—we need to recognize the inner states we don't like or avoid and shunt into dark corners, because this is where our greatest opportunities exist.

Despair becomes a jewel of many facets, some of which shine as faith and trust. On the other side of the iron coin of terror is where freedom lives, where we find that real fearlessness is not about having no fear, but about having fierce courage in the face of fear. Feelings of failure and disappointment can melt into the strength of resilience or a rebirth of creativity. The driven need to rigidly control can relax and expand into an open field of wise vulnerability. Anger metamorphs into clarity. Anxiety gives way to inner strength. New skills and capacities begin to grow within us.

RELAX INTO EMPTINESS

If we are to realize our full potential as human beings, we can and must make friends with the reality of inner emptiness. Pondering reality as it is in a contemplative way we can mine the caverns of inner emptiness for jewels of many kinds. Rather than being the victim of our own fear and sliding into debilitating and unproductive bouts of the D times, we can learn that the whole process is a gift. When we cultivate this perspective, we may be surprised by spontaneous feelings of gratitude.

We can begin by noticing how we avoid emptiness. Sometimes we sense the echo of inner emptiness in lapses of silence in conversations, which we quickly cover up with idle chatter or social nicety. We buffer ourselves against emptiness with addictions and compulsions. We dread being alone. We fill every moment of silence with noise.

Once we've discovered how it is with us and "the void," then we can gather up our courage and begin to cultivate a relationship with emptiness as a personal ally. The important practice of formal meditation is a famous entryway to working with emptiness. Both meditation and contemplation give ample opportunities to notice the way thoughts and emotions come and go, so that we catch a glimpse of how their basic nature is fleeting and empty. Even while we are being active, we can build a capacity for inner stillness and listening within our own silence. There, in the inner world, we sense into the freedom and creative impulse that arises from inner space.

In contemplation, meditation and prayer, the deep self is at ease with perceiving and resting in emptiness or the feeling of nonexistence. The self can let go and be nothing precisely because it is also everything. The Hindu traditions speak of vast cycles of time and space, being and non-being, when the self or being disappears into emptiness or non-being. The seed of being re-emerges in the next cycle of divine love, the Supreme Reality outpouring itself to bring Creation to life—from unity to multiplicity and back to unity again in spirals of becoming. Allowing the experience of inner emptiness into our awareness can help to relax the conditioned fears of the surface self and give us a taste of the equanimity that we long for.

> *For the world and time are the dance of the Lord in emptiness. The silence of the spheres is the music of a wedding feast. The more we persist in misunderstanding the phenomena of life, the more we analyze them out into strange finalities and complex purposes of our own, the more we involve ourselves in sadness, absurdity, and despair. But it does not matter much, because no despair of ours can alter the reality of things, or stain the joy of the cosmic dance which is always there. Indeed, we are in the midst of it, and it is in the midst of us, for it beats in our very blood, whether we want it or not.*
>
> —Thomas Merton

Empty and full. Emptiness wouldn't exist without fullness— another pair of opposites that provide a rich field for the play of consciousness. We can enjoy high times of laughter and festivity and action even more when we surrender into times of simplicity, solitude, silence…and emptiness. For no matter how hard we may try to avoid emptiness, the evolutionary force of the self will push the personality (who we continue to believe ourselves to be) toward a breakthrough or reunion with all the displaced, denied parts of ourselves that have been made outcast by our fears.

Emptiness is a great teacher—one that lives within us and is a natural dimension of our own being. We have to discover for ourselves whether or not the Buddhists are right when they say that "emptiness is like a glass filled with sunlight." Out of that rich, luminous, mysterious space, life is roused, whether it moves toward stillness and peace or toward creative expression. Becoming familiar with emptiness builds inner strength and resilience that will serve us well when despair and doubt come to stay for a while.

> Quickly, a storm is coming!
> Take shelter in the sanctuary
> of solitude and silence.
> Be ready with an empty cup
> for the deluge of reality
> in such somber bloody times,
> be ready for the shower of gold
> that waters the soul, because
> there are no words
> to describe such beauty
> falling from the hands of God.

SEEK AND GIVE SANCTUARY

We all need sanctuary, and ultimately the sanctuary we crave is within us. There are as many ways to take refuge in sanctuary as there are individuals. It's a process that is unique to each person. Gratitude for all the gifts of life and for the fact that we are alive is one of the most essential inroads to the sanctuary within, and it can be cultivated. The difficult times we face may be our greatest opportunity to discover that inner refuge, and while that's where we find the source of sanctuary, contemplation includes taking action in the world outside ourselves.

The Refuge of Trees

Find a tree that draws you to it. Look at it. Appreciate the beauty of its form, how its limbs reach toward the sky, notice the patterns of its leaves. After you've taken it in visually, go and sit with it, lean against its solid strength, rest in its shade, feel into the earth and water of it, listen to its sounds as the wind threshes its leaves.

Call to mind what you know about the roots of trees, how most of the tree is underground and connected to everything around it. Botanists now know that trees transmit information to each other through their roots as well as through their leaves. Remember, as well, what you know of photosynthesis and ponder the miracle of how trees turn light into leaves, spirit into matter. Dwell upon trees as the source of the oxygen we breathe. Let the tree be with you, speak to you in some way. Trees bring me ease and peace of mind. Most trees are amazingly compassionate beings. The cynic in us might call this being a "tree-hugger." Actually, it is a simple and profound contemplation of nature.

As much as the D-times are the soul's way of calling us to the inner life, they may also be times when we are called to action that is carried on the wings of contemplation. When feeling disconnected from your own source of sanctuary, the action of serving others in some way can be a great solace. Even the simple act of listening with compassion to a friend in need or offering a helping hand in some way can be contemplation in action. Taking the time to visit an aging parent or grandparent can be a profound act of kindness and generosity. Contemplation builds the virtue of empathy. Opening up in this way makes us more able to be with children at play in their world of present time, or to sit at the bedside of a dying loved one in silent communion, heart to heart.

Cultivating gratitude leads to generosity and natural empathy. Serving others brings out the generous spirit of empathy, which creates space for kindness and compassion to flow. Generosity is healing for the one who gives. When we become a sanctuary or refuge for others, we receive the same in return and beyond. In the contemplative act of serving another, we can discover that service itself is truly a form of contemplation.

Give your creativity free rein. Creativity is a life raft that keeps me afloat, even as dark waters churn and careen. Creativity has a brightening and uplifting effect, takes me out of obsession and transforms my emotions into pure energy. Creativity is magical; it moves toward a mystery of the soul. Creativity and the native *sahaja* of the self walk hand in hand.

Creative expression in all forms is another powerful way to work with the D's. Knowing that it's not necessarily going to "cure" me of my depression or agitation, I throw my full attention and five senses into creative expression. But then, I'm not looking for a cure. I'm trusting the process of my inner yoga and looking for a useful, benevolent and practical place to ground my attention.

Writing that journal piece or blog or book chapter, gardening, playing or listening to music, or cooking tonight's dinner and feeding a friend—once your attention is on the creative act, it just might inspire or spontaneously propel you into a different mood. It's a fact of life that what we focus on is what we get, so let's have some intention about what we allow ourselves to focus on, day in and day out.

Back in April 2020 when I first declared for myself, "This is depression," I started writing journal entries on my computer. I cooked wonderful food (the kitchen is one of my favorite places for contemplation), chanted and sang songs. I began to correspond with friends by email, meeting on the internet through programs like Zoom, looking for ways to connect and be of service to others. Suddenly I was engaged in a flow of life that was bigger than my despair. It's not that sadness and grief went away, but they took a back seat. From the driver's seat, I could turn and acknowledge their presence in my vehicle at any time. I could hear and sometimes sing the song of their heartfelt lament.

I revisited a project that had been gathering some dust—writing my third novel in a series of historical fiction near and dear to my heart. I started researching the era of the story, contemplating my characters and their arcs of experience. I became fascinated with the Celtic world of ancient Briton and the Roman-dominated south of France, where legend says that Mary Magdalene went into exile with Joseph of Arimathea and a small group of disciples. History has a way of showing us that adversity and political upheaval have always been a part of the human experience. One night I laughed with my husband, saying, "You know, this probably isn't our first plague!"

Back to nature. Sheltering in place, as I pondered depression back in the spring of 2020, nature was my first source of refuge. At early morning and at twilight I found sanctuary in the beauty of nature and the strange, buoyant joy that sometimes bubbled up in me. The rhythms of sun and moon reassured me, as did the pine trees around my cottage. Visiting bobcats brought the gift of delight. I spent as much time as possible outside in between stints at the computer. I went for walks, watched springtime arrive despite it all. It was two months before I was finally able to go to the piano. But I was able to write and sing. And I was able to pray, because the D-times are those moments that bring me to my knees.

Eventually, in the wedding bed of creative expression, grace lifted me up. Another old friend, gratitude, started seeping through the cracks in my heart in quiet moments. Inner resources of courage and resilience came forward, easily accessible. Wild sunflowers, which I had planted as seeds harvested back in the fall of 2019, grew prolifically into a thick patch of tall, waving green guardians around the northern flank of my cottage. They began to bloom in bursts of golden yellow, drawing finches, bees and butterflies, while my recalcitrant salvia bushes came to life and were soon covered with small, deep-red or violet blossoms. It was all happening in perfect sync with my inner state.

Thankfully, no matter how dark the night, the dawn always comes. No matter how deeply we descend, when we let ourselves go through the full process of transformation, there is eventually an ascent. That's how impermanence teaches trust in the process of life—by showing us that "this too shall pass." At any time, grace may take us, and our sadness and anger, despair and depression will melt into the seedbed of the soul, coming back to germinate and flourish in the garden bowers of reverie, intuitive knowing and thanksgiving. Reveling in the beauty all around us, a moment of contemplation opens the heart.

In early September a large band of wild javelinas—swarthy, pig-like desert animals akin to deer—came through looking for food and water. They completely ravaged my beautiful wild sunflowers, stripping the tall, sturdy stalks of flowers and leaves. Only the topmost of each branch was left with a shred of life. It was nature at its finest, showing me the transitory nature of all that is beautiful, reminding me to honor my feelings of loss and the sadness that comes with it.

Somewhere in the dance between impermanence and fleeting beauty, we will meet grief, which has its own power to transform. Years ago, when my partner of twenty years died, I learned that grief is a spiritual enzyme that can catalyze deep transformations over time, if we surrender ourselves to feel it all. Surfing the seething, foamy, inrushing waves of our D-times or floating their currents out to sea, we may be surprised by grace, finding that the dark salt waters of loss, grief, love and beauty may wash us back to shore again, but changed.

VII

Inspired Flow

You know how the air becomes rarified when the storm of loss blows through? Charged with light. A gleaming border surrounding every leaf and eyelash. An electrical current bathing your spine as you shop for peaches and unclip the laundry from the line. As if you had been turned inside out by the darkness, rendered exquisitely singular. Almost chosen, like a prophet or a princess. And how the rest of the world goes on in its inane everydayness, oblivious to the sanctity of the broken-open sky in which you now abide?
—Mirabai Starr

Creative vision belongs only to him who, without being stopped by the dance of life, dares to look within himself as far as the Void. Then what does he see? The beginning and the end—that is to say the seed from which life springs and the flowers under which life's adventure ends. He sees the rainbow of the Void linking them both.
—Sri Anirvan

"Eternity is in love with the creations of time." This much-loved quote from the English philosopher-poet William Blake (1757-1827) speaks to the relationship between creativity and the soul. The timeless flow that happens for us, creatures existing in time, is the place in the human soul where creativity is born. The current of life flows eternally within each and every one of us. We only have to tap into it. That flow is what fuels the imaginative spirit and links us to creativity in every form and expression.

Imagination is closely linked with the intelligence of the heart and is activated and super-charged in the many moods of contemplation. As the Baul mystic yogi, Sri Anirvan, writes, it's in the "rainbow of the Void" that links the beginning and the end, the dark and the light, the good and the bad, the joy and the sorrow, that we discover the mysterious river of flow that is underlying all of space and time. Letting go into the open space of the inner world, imagination may be tender and hesitant at first. Our imaginative faculty has been roughed-up, pushed away, downtrodden, denied... possibly for years. At any time in our lives, imagination can be awakened from its slumber. It's a lot like pumping a well to bring up the source water. We must coax the gentle, delicate world of imagination to come to visit us.

As soon as imagination (aka the "Muse") knows that she's really welcome, she will come flooding in and make herself at home, because she's just been waiting for you. Once she's invited into your world, she'll take over with her transforming influence, bringing creativity with her. It's a takeover that is welcomed, for when the caravan of the Muse arrives, she's laden with gifts and surprises to lay at your feet.

ROMANCE THE MUSE

The power to create was imagined in the ancient Greek culture as the nine Muses, all of them beautiful women of differing temperaments and gifts. Being a woman myself, I know that she likes to be romanced, to have attention on her. She likes a beautiful space, the fragrance of a rose or a bouquet of summer flowers. She likes to be asked to dance, to laugh and be playful. She loves music. She's colorful, wild and lush, though she can be fierce and austere as well. Sometimes she's the simplicity of one note, one hue, one word…or silence itself.

The Muse hides when I'm furious or self-deprecating and becomes hesitant when I'm insecure. She basks in the warm and gracious mood of trust. She responds to the confidence and freedom of a spacious personality that can let go of concepts and "shoulds." She enjoys love in all its moods and expressions. She is sensual in every way and rises up as joy in the human body. She deeply appreciates generosity. She moves by the spirit of the law and she stops dead in her tracks at the letter of the law. She dances lightly through change and is exalted when she's carried by the flow of life.

Her dwelling place is the heart. She is merciful and full of grace. She embraces us with all of our worries, fears, doubts and flaws. The Muse only asks that we be honest and present with what is, whatever it is. It is this full trust and acceptance that opens the floodgates of the moment.

I recently saw the movie "All Is True," about the life of William Shakespeare, a genius of awesome scope. In one scene, he is working in his garden when a young stranger walks by and stops for a chat. Realizing that the gardener is none other than the famous playwright and poet, he seeks advice about how to be a writer. He wonders, how did Shakespeare navigate "the geography of the soul" and write all of those amazing plays that took place in Italy or Scotland, or on a ship sailing across the Atlantic…when in fact he never left England?

Shakespeare answered the young man's question: "The best way to be a writer is to start writing," he began. "What I know, if I know, I have imagined…. If you want to be a writer and speak to others and for others, speak first for yourself. Search within. Consider the contents of your own soul, your humanity, and if you're honest with yourself, then, whatever you write, *all…is… true!*" Wise words and sage advice.

Writers of novels often say that when the creative imagination takes over, the characters come to life and live themselves. It's an amazing feeling when the book begins to write itself, one of the reasons I'm passionate about writing fiction these days. That mysterious flow is the Muse at work. The artist Pablo Picasso once said, "Everything you can imagine is real." Genius physicist Albert Einstein had many things to say about imagination as well:

I am enough of an artist to draw freely upon my imagination.

Imagination is more important than knowledge. Knowledge is limited. Imagination encircles the world.

Imagination is everything. It is the preview of life's coming attractions.

Being true to yourself is at the core of contemplative life and its creative expressions. This is something I've learned time and again. The Muse knows the difference between what is real and what is unreal, including and especially in you. The Muse knows your deepest, truest, and often hidden longings.

Try giving your imagination full permission to see your hidden potentials. When you find yourself up against a wall of resistance or pain is a good time to experiment. To begin, just stay with the familiar felt sense of the wall or flood of emotion. Greet it like a friend, if you can, not trying to force a breakthrough or change. Keep letting go of any self-judging that comes up. Relax. Breathe.

Be simple and easy with yourself as you imagine: What if your cloying past, painful memories, baggage and restraints suddenly melted away, like mist in the morning sun? If all that was no longer present, even for just a few moments, who would you be? What could become possible? If you need a place to start, reflect on these questions: *How could my life be different? What creativity do I want to express? What freedom calls to me?*

Feel free to write, if you like, as you visualize your life in full color, like a movie, and imagine how you might evolve during the next year...then, in five years. This is a moment to let imagination have its play. Use your sense of sight and seeing. Let yourself go there, fully, without censoring or being stopped by your limitations. Write in fragments and single words or in full sentences. Opening the door of the imagination, even a little, can give a glimpse of true purpose, those quiet impulses of the soul that move us incrementally (and sometimes swiftly) in the direction of becoming who we are meant to be.

GENTLE, BRIGHT AND FLEXIBLE

Transformation is what the creative imagination is all about. The key that opens the doors to imagination is found in a feminine approach that yields what Cynthia Bourgeault calls "the luminous seeing of contemplation." This inner yoga is not about women or a woman. It's about the feminine aspect in both man and woman—that which is receptive, empathetic, open-hearted. Over thirty years ago my teacher, Lee, wrote:

> *The process is feminine, and the keys to the lock that imprisons Reality or Truth are in a feminine approach. We must go at this knot of confusion called the mind or sleep—or unconsciousness, illusion or maya—with a very gentle, humorous, patient, accepting relationship*

to it. We can practice vigorously but with bright and
flexible vigor—not rigid, righteous vigor.

We must give ourselves time to relax into this enlighten-
ment, whatever it is, rather than trying to force it to take us over,
permeate our fears and illusions, which of course it cannot do!
Beyond the obvious, which is actually to realize that which we
seek, if we approach this work as Woman, we may just discover
something quite unexpected, surprising, and delightful.

The road to personal transformation through creativity is not a forced march or a strong-armed effort. Creativity needs the discipline of the warrior spirit, with its clarity and strength of purpose and determination. Warriorship is one of life's many gifts, but too much fire will burn the tender heart, sometimes with disastrous effects. Imagination calls for a different kind of warrior. In his groundbreaking book, *Shambhala: Sacred Path of the Warrior*, the late Tibetan Buddhist teacher, Chögyam Trungpa Rinpoche, described the tender and vulnerable heart of a warrior who conquers not through aggression or violence but through gentleness, compassion, and self-knowledge—with a "bright and flexible vigor."

Every human being needs a full measure of loving kindness and generosity. We need relaxation and acceptance to open up the tender places of the heart. It's the feminine principle that rules in this domain—from earthly mother to cosmic mother—though she certainly does have a fierce warrior side as well. As author Mirabai Starr writes in her book, *Wild Mercy*, "I believe in the healing energy of the feminine as a fire that can melt the frozen heart of the world, the artistry that will mend the tattered web of interconnection."

The inner yoga of imagination and creativity employs the feminine, right side of the brain that is intuitive, highly plastic and generative. Creativity needs a lot of free space in which to play and roam, bringing us back to the fifth element of Samkhya philosophy, space—the "mother" or matrix in which the other four elements have life. We've come full circle to where we started with one of the most basic purposes of contemplation: to create spaciousness within us and, in doing so, to craft the spacious person that we can be.

Both outer and inner space is a gift of the feminine that generates and supports relaxation, rejuvenation, reverie and effortless creative flow. At deeper levels of transformation, the feminine aspect of our own being can unfurl into the sweetness of trust, wise innocence and inner peace, even when times get tough. When we have enough inner space for the creative feminine to arise and move and dance freely with whatever is present in our lives, we enter into the art of contemplation.

Listening within for the natural movements of the soul, what is arising spontaneously? There is an urge, something that pushes just a little, the tiniest movement like the tip of a growing plant reaching toward the sun. Do you sense it? Perhaps you are moved toward a musical instrument, your garage, kitchen, writing desk or studio. You pick up the brush and the paints and go to the canvas or arrange the ingredients of the meal you will cook with care and loving attention to detail. There is nothing forced about this contemplative activity. Drifting effortlessly on a current, awareness is both focused and diffuse at the same time. You may have a destination in mind, but you do not know the way. You simply follow the flow, knowing it will be revealed to you as you go.

My teacher used to say that the transformational potential of creativity lies in the mood that arises in the process of speaking, writing, singing, building, cooking, planting a garden, sculpting, painting. We can bring the same mood and soulful spirit to whatever we are doing, until we are carried along on the current of the river.

GET IN THE FLOW

There are many ways to get into the creative state of flow. Some people get into that wonderful state of being in their woodshop, or working with numbers, landscaping a garden, or using hands to heal others. For others, the fast way to flow is through activity like mountain climbing, running, walking or yoga. While I love to walk, my personal fast road to flow happens in other ways. On some mornings I'm moved to pull out the piano bench and sit down to play whatever comes. The mood is quiet, intent yet relaxed, so that I have the sense of being both purposeful and at ease. Depending on where my hands want to go, I start in the key of D or in C or A in the major or the minor mode, which has everything to do with the tone of my mood. If I'm a bit sad or wistful, I play in the minor mode. If I'm filled with gladness and verve, it's the mood of the major keys that move me. Playing the piano in any mood is spontaneous and vivid, and it nourishes my soul. But I wasn't always able to do that—it's a skill I've crafted over decades of my adult life.

One of the formative stories of my life is about how I stopped playing the piano at age ten. One day my mother told me that my father was coming to visit the house where we had lived with my grandparents since I was three years old. I was so excited! I'd been a "father orphan" as long as I could remember. My father was alive, though he never wrote or sent a birthday card. My mother, grandparents, aunts and uncles wouldn't talk about him other than to say that Walt lived in Virginia.

Their silence spoke volumes that I couldn't understand, but even so, I was excited to see the person who was my dad. Turned out I was like the other kids—I actually had one. Secretly, hope sprang to life in the innocent mind and heart of a child. Oblivious to the tension between my mother and father, I sat with them in the living room until my mother got up to make coffee. Eager for my father's love, I almost bounced with energy as I went to the old upright piano, pulled out the worn wooden bench, and played.

"Stop that," he snapped after a few short moments. "You're making too much noise."

Surprised, I turned and looked at him. "But I want to play for you."

He turned away and watched as my mother came in with a tray in hand. "That's enough. Now go and play somewhere else. I want to talk to your mother."

Tears stinging my eyes, feeling ashamed, I went to the back yard, my refuge at all times, and cried beneath the magnolia tree.

When I returned, he was standing on the porch to leave. He barely spoke to me, and to this day I have no memory of a goodbye hug or even a smile.

Unaware of what had happened between my father and me, my mother didn't say much about him, just that he'd gone back to Virginia. Soon after that time I stopped practicing the piano, and it fell away from my life. Two years later, I took up guitar and by the time I was thirteen, I was singing Joan Baez folk songs.

When I was sixteen years old, I asked my mother to explain what had happened that day. She told me that he had come to ask if there was any possibility of a reunion between them. "I'm different now," he said. But she and her daughters had received too much of his violence and anger after he came back from the firing lines of the war in 1945. She'd made a tough decision long ago, and, for my mother, there was no turning back. Seeing from the vantage point of many years, I know that she made the right decision for us all.

My brilliant, handsome, and emotionally wounded father resurfaced in my life four years later. We got to know each other, made our peace, and parted with a measure of love and acceptance when he died of cancer years later, but that's another long story. When I turned thirty, I began to yearn to play the piano. I could not shake the feeling that I should be playing Mozart, Chopin, blues and boogie-woogie, as if it was a part of the blueprint with which I was born. Looking back over my life, I could see when and how I'd made the decision to stop playing the piano.

I spent some time grieving the loss of my own creativity. Then, one day when I was visiting my mother in Louisiana, I spoke about the sadness I felt. She listened closely to my story of what happened that day when I was ten. Then she took me to her organ (she played for the tiny rural church nearby) in the living room.

"You can still play," she reassured me, her rich alto voice reverberating with loving encouragement. "I'll show you the basics of playing by ear, using both hands, treble and bass." I spent the next forty years experimenting and embellishing, based upon that one instruction. Today, I have such deep gratitude for that wonderful, healing moment at the organ with her.

Even though there's an old scar, a trauma of a kind, I play around my limitations—and maybe even because of them. Letting the keys resound with the melodies that please my ear, sometimes I sense that my mother and grandmother, both piano players, and especially my great-grandmother, who played piano and violin with the New Orleans Symphony orchestra over a hundred years ago, are helping and blessing me.

We've all got poignant stories from childhood. What I learned from this part of mine is that I don't have to be Beethoven to enjoy playing the piano and get into flow. This is true of every form of creativity. The experience of flow is not reserved for special, lucky or extraordinarily gifted people. Effortless flow happens for ordinary people in ordinary circumstances when the critical, analytical mind is surpassed by body and soul. It's a moment when heaven joins earth, and a wash of rejuvenating energy is unleashed.

One of my favorite ways to get into flow through contemplative music is with the *ektara*, a simple, one-stringed folk instrument of the Bauls, the wandering mystic yogis of Bengal and northern India who revere the human potential of innate sahaja. The handmade *ektara* is the polar opposite of a complex instrument like the piano, but it is extraordinary in its simplicity. With the first touch of a finger on the single string, the simplicity of the ektara invokes a profound and deep *bhavana*, or contemplative mood. The one note symbolizes unity and oneness, while the voice can take flight with intricate melodies and rhapsodies of song. Over the years I've collected many ektaras, but the one I love the most was made in Bengal and given to me by my friend, the amazing singer, practitioner and spiritual teacher, Parvathy Baul, who is a living example of creativity as contemplation and prayer.

Creativity and imagination can be tapped in any life-positive activity. For me, writing has been an enduring doorway to creative flow. When I was younger, I could spend ten hours a day writing. Now, to support my health, I have to limit my hours sitting at a computer. I get up and stretch or go for short walks during a day of writing. I cook, listen to music, exercise or even dance a little in between hours at the computer. Life has a way of asking us to work with our limitations, and in that way we are tempered and softened. That beautiful flow is still available to me as the writer I am now, and I go there to meet the Muse as often as I can. If you are so moved, try the writing exercise that follows.

CONTEMPLATIVE WRITING

Pick up a notebook or journal and a pen. Go outside and find a comfortable place to sit. Maybe you want a pillow to support your back. Paying attention to your breath, relax and let go of your plans and "to do" list. Now, look at the sky. Let yourself gaze, unfettered, free of expectations or any specific goal of what should be right now.

Notice how the natural world is moving and changing, in the wind or in the quality of the light. What do you see about the sky? Is it wide open, an empty bowl of blue, or are there clouds? If there are clouds, are they moving or still? Be aware of the air or the caress of wind on your skin, how it moves the trees and plants around you. See how the sun illumines the world. Is it honey colored, dusky, golden, or bright yellow like lemons? Is it morning, midday, or sunset?

If you can't go outside, get comfortable in your home. Observe whatever is around you, maybe a couch, a chair, refrigerator, bookcase, bed, paintings or sculptures, plants, a dining table and chairs. Pay attention to the smells that drift on the air. Is incense burning or dinner cooking on the stove? What is the quality of the light here, inside? Is it filtered sunlight coming through a window, the glow of a candle, the shine of an electric bulb? If you can look out a window, what do you see? Just *seeing* images of nature can catalyze a whole range of impressions and bring us into relationship with the greater world.

Whether you're inside or outside, pay special attention to the space between the objects. How do space and light reflect your inner state? Sense into how you are connected to everything around you through space. Breathe in the air that exists within that space. Let space speak to you through silence.

Now, with pen in hand, free write whatever comes to you. Let yourself be sensual. Use your senses to perceive reality as it appears to you here and now. You can use description to connect with the world around you. What do you feel and see? Let yourself free associate, allowing the mind to roam over images and see where they take you. Every image has a symbolic power. Trust yourself. Go with it. Pay attention to how you're breathing...and keep breathing. Be easy. Let yourself flow.

Writing for yourself is a very useful form of contemplation. Surrender to your own voice, listening to what you have to say. Let your writing lead you where it wants to go. Opposite emotions often co-exist. I'm depressed, but at the same time I'm grateful— or, I'm sad even while I notice a small, upwelling spring of hidden joy. Write what is true for you.

In this time of retreat and seclusion, when we are wrestling with the pandemic as well as with the glaring light it has shown on the urgent situation of humanity on so many fronts, writing is one of the ways I stay grounded. Whatever you write, you may find that, in giving your imagination and your voice full rein, you are changed in some way by having written the truth.

Touching the real in this way, we may contact, even for a second, our own deep nature and the delight and wise innocence that is so often veiled and hidden from our experience. As much as I love the formless mystery, I love also the world of form. I enjoy describing my love, because the more I put my attention on that which I love, the more alive and vivid and nourishing it becomes.

What about you? *How, when, where and what inspires and catalyzes your inner connection in the flow state?* Start your inquiry with what opens the heart, because the open heart will lead you to flow faster than anything else.

VIII

Gratitude and Grace

It is necessary to praise life by how we carry out everything we do
and wonder about. That way the world will not die.
—Martin Prechtel

The immediate expression of the Divine is love. It manifests only as
love, selfless love. Love for love's sake, not love for any motive.
—Ma Devaki

I realize it is more than a lot to ask of you, this Sacred Way. I ask
nonetheless. I am very anxious. I have seen the coming times.
It is not only that you need God, it is that we need one another.
Need! Not even as food or shelter but as deeply, more deeply, than the
very air we breathe. You must consider Loving God in an organic,
total way or life has no meaning. This I know—heart, flesh, blood,
and soul, chemically and cellularly. Existence is meaningless
if you don't reach the Heart of God.
—Lee Lozowick

In contemplation, the inner plane of our being will lead us to dwell on everything that concerns the heart—what the heart feels, what the heart imagines, what the heart knows, and the love that moves the heart—while it also teaches us to let go and trust. Opening the heart is about being true to what contemplation reveals to us. When the heart awakens, we can no longer betray ourselves, what we have known, seen and felt. Greeting life with an open heart in all circumstances is how we come to know the gateways of the heart. It's how we can learn that which is worthy of our devotion.

DEVOTION

What does it mean to be a devotee? "To devote" is to give or apply one's time, attention or self (or all three) to a purpose or pursuit. In devotion we dedicate ourselves to giving careful attention to what is meaningful to us. We give the gift of ourselves.

The deep self yearns to be a devotee of the Sacred, because that is its natural state of being. The journey to reach the "Heart of God," however that mystery is real for you, already exists in the archetypal blueprint of human beings. It's a long and winding road to become who we are. Many people call it the spiritual path, and it is a path of transformation.

What asks for your devotion? You can feel it in deep conversation with an aging parent or a dear friend. Devotion can be present in the kitchen, at the computer, at the potter's wheel, at the weaver's loom, in the office, when we take our kids on a camping trip. Devotion moves the work of a business deal that will profit everyone concerned in positive ways. I think of my friend, an archeologist. whose business represents the concerns of First Nation tribes in negotiations with industry and government by documenting burial grounds and other aspects of the sacred landscape. He is devoted to his work and intensely inspired by it.

Devotion is the fuel that moves what we love to do. Offering or teaching something—music, hatha yoga, creative writing, meditation or mindfulness—that inspires and benefits others is a powerful act of devotion. Singing in a choir, or helping others learn how to sing. Getting involved with your local community in all kinds of ways. Working with hospice and giving your tender heart to those who are dying.

BEAUTY

The art of contemplation bears the fruit of an awakened heart, but we will find that we need to stay engaged in the process to keep it open. Contemplation is a way of life, not a one-time deal or a limited engagement. Once we have tasted the sweetness of the inner life, we will find that we are hungry for its nectar, yearning for its illuminating light, longing for another glimpse of its beauty. We keep the doorway open by staying in touch with our own sacred vulnerability and brokenheartedness, so that the river of our feeling flows unimpeded and the fire of our clarity burns bright.

Beauty, found everywhere in Creation, is a gateway to the heart. And so we seek beauty in all things. The awakened heart may lead to what the Bauls and Indian mystics call *bhava*, divine mood, and *rasa*, divine feeling or nectar. These are moods permeated with beauty and reverence. Seeking beauty we will find it, in the eyes of a child, in the soft, veined hands of the very old, in volcanoes and tornados, in the words of the poets who move us to flights of the soul. We hear it in the symphony, hymn, gospel song, rock ballad or Sanskrit chant, in art of all kinds. We experience it in the dancers and the drum at a Native American pow-wow. There are endless forms of beauty that have the power to make cracks in our once-stony hearts now made tender; cracks where divine love flows through to wash everyone and everything in its healing power.

Cultivating inner beauty and moods of devotion go hand in hand. Our gratitude leads us to see beauty everywhere, and beauty inspires more gratitude. Encouraged by beauty, we may be moved to just sit quietly and bask in such a mood. As the saying goes, an image is worth a thousand words. We might imagine a beautiful garden where we dwell with our Beloved. Using your feminine, heartfelt faculty of imagination, you can create an inner sanctuary, an inner room or temple or garden of the heart, where you offer love and devotion, take refuge, and seek blessings and help from the deity, divinity, guides or revered teachers of your particular path. In whatever way devotion calls to you, open your heart to love.

Seeking beauty, the individual heart itself becomes beautiful. Beauty opens the doors of my longing, makes me aware of the Supreme Reality. These are subtle inner experiences, unique to each person. It's those moments of sacred mood and devotion that draw the attention of deities and heavenly beings. We might encounter mandalas of light, beings such as Tara, Saraswati, Mary, Jesus, Krishna, Buddha—or a wordless reunion with the benevolent universal oneness that awaits us within.

GRACE AND MERCY

In the contemplative life, as we acknowledge and work to transform the darkness within and around us, the heart awakens naturally to the divine grace that is everywhere, causing the light of our being to shine brighter. We begin to see and connect with creative solutions to the problems of the world and the emerging sense of oneness in humanity. Sustained by beauty and the gracious spirit of the Sacred permeating all things, we might discover that the mercy of grace is ever-present.

As our awareness becomes rooted in what is real, we live from the depths of the feeling and knowing human heart that is transparent and receptive to the reality of grace. As the inner self gives purpose to the outer self, we are led down many roads through acceptance and on toward trust and surrender. When we surrender to the truth of oneness, of divinity, we make space for grace to take over. The lure of our own longing will lead us on the journey and, as we contemplate our way through space-time, wonder and awe give rise to praise.

The awakened heart of gratitude and compassion is the true life, which makes our words and deeds eloquent, strong and empowered. They ring with the truth and carry the power to heal and restore. Our praise leads back again to prayer. The soul calls for these mysteries, for silence, stillness, rapture, reverie, wonder and the gratitude that nourishes our personhood, while we also feed the soul of the world.

There is always more to say and to discover about the art of contemplation. I leave that intimate exploration to you, dear reader—to the thick, wild regions of your own heart. Just one last thing: Regardless of what we do or what we believe, we all serve something in this life. Each one of us has an innate sense of purpose. We have the power to make a choice...who, what, when, where, and how we will serve.

We can choose to serve the luxuriant, mysterious gift of Creation. We can choose to devote our lives in praise of the Supreme Reality alive in the world as faith, gratitude, beauty, majesty, mercy. We can choose to actively contemplate and praise the immanent divinity and oneness residing in all beings and things. It's a choice that might lead to finding "grace and mercy in Her wild hair," as the poet Ramprasad Sen once wrote of the goddess Kali—because the power of grace is the pinnacle of Creation, and in that sense, grace is the feminine side of divinity who is mother and father, lover and friend, dual and nondual. That's a sweeping statement, and I cherish the vast scope of it. It's a big palette, an infinite playground in which grace can have her way with us, as she brings us through it all to dwell at the heart of the world. May it be so. *Tathastu.*

Surely life has a beautiful meaning and purpose when it is understood to be of an universal nature and significance. The utmost grandeur of it is revealed when it breaks through every sense of division and diversity, and sheds all around soothing light of pure, spontaneous love—the rapture of an inexplicable joy and peace.

—Swami Ramdas

EPILOGUE

Hear the Wild Bird Sing

Nearly three billion birds have disappeared across North America since 1970, a decline of twenty-nine percent, while two-thirds of all bird species are at risk of extinction due to climate change. Another fact: Traffic noise is known to disrupt bird songs.

May 2020. A few days ago, I was out walking just before sunset when my attention was captured by the sweet songs of a solitary bird. I stopped to listen as a repertoire of trills, chirrups and tweets came forth in an aria of birdsong. Gazing toward the horizon, I saw that the purple mountains in the west were tipped with molten gold where the blazing disc of the sun hovered and would soon disappear. Scanning, I located one small, ordinary grey and white bird sitting at the top of a tall juniper tree, facing the setting sun and singing its heart out for the end of the day.

For many years during my summers in Europe, I was carried away at dawn and dusk by the sounds of wild birds singing on the country ashram where I lived. The songs of black birds were especially thrilling, and, in particular, a famous plain brown bird that can produce up to one thousand different sounds…the nightingale. This fascinating wonder of the avian world is unique for many reasons. With a vast migratory pattern, nightingales arrive in Europe from Africa, where they have wintered over. They can be heard in France and Germany in the spring and early summer, before they fly further north when it begins to get hot.

Their famous, poetic name, "nightingale," makes it sound like they sing at night. It's true that I usually heard them at twilight, either dawn or dusk. It turns out that the males do sing at night to draw the attention of females who might be flying overhead.

In the high desert of Arizona, there are many birds that sing beautifully, like the red-wing blackbirds that live in the cottonwood trees along the Verde River. But up here in the mesas, it's the mockingbird that intoxicates. Unlike European nightingales, these hardy desert songsters have only two hundred different songs, all lifted from other avian species. Like nightingales, the North American mockingbird is a fabulous mimic who "mocks" by putting it all together in a glorious burst of song. And as Ernest Hemingway (a favorite writer and inspiration) once said, "You're allowed to steal anything if you can make it better."

By now you may be wondering where I'm going with this contemplation on birdsong. Stay with me, we are going somewhere. On this particular evening I was contemplating the global pandemic, which may be our most recent sign of "the end of the world as we know it" along with extreme climate change, the toxicity of our life-giving oceans, satellite debris orbiting Earth, the extinction of species, extreme deforestation, and proliferating violence.

Mythologizing, which I am prone to do, demands lucent, lambent symbols. My mellifluous desert bird singing to the setting sun is a good one. What does it mean to sing at the moment when the light fades into darkness? Why do blackbirds—those awesome divas—sing in the dead of night? (Thanks to poets John Lennon and Paul McCartney.)

I find these to be metaphors worth pondering. And the poetry of my ponder goes like this: The wild bird sings until the last moment of the day and even in the dead of night because it spontaneously expresses its innate nature, which is to sing. Does a bird's instinct "know" that the sun, which inspires its song, never goes away but disappears for a duration before it returns?

Poised as we are at the point of no return on our beautiful blue planet, and knowing that life goes on no matter what happens, how do we choose to work with the time that we are given to live? Will we keep singing as the long day of our epoch comes to an end? Will we sing and keep singing, until we can sing no more?

When I listened to the mockingbird's melodies that evening, my heart was uplifted. My grey bird sang for all the endings I have known and have yet to know, and for the beginning of what is unknown. Praise for all that is sacred in life was the *rasa*, the juice, the nectar of that voice. His cry to heaven invoked praise in me, as the horizon turned golden and the sunset sky was streaked with rosy puffs and deep orange fountains and mansions of cirrus and cumulus clouds.

Walking back to my cottage, I sat outside to watch as the day faded into night and the greater cosmos came into view. First there was the gloaming, then a goddess appeared—Venus, the evening star. Slowly, other planetary luminaries began to shine, foretelling the ponderous miracle of the Milky Way and infinite distant brilliant suns that bejeweled the vast dark spread of space.

Finally, night gave way to sleep and the coming of dawn. The sun rose, as it always does (until it eventually explodes in a final last gasp of glory), and another day began, when I would ponder again the irrepressible joy I feel whenever the wild bird sings.

Recommended Reading

Allione, Lama Tsultrim, *Wisdom Rising: Journey into the Mandala of the Empowered Feminine*, 2018.

Anirvan, Sri & Lizelle Raymond, *To Live Within: Teachings of a Baul*, 1984.

Beresford-Kroeger, Diana, *To Speak for the Trees*, 2019.

Bly, Robert & Marion Woodman, *The Maiden King: The Reunion of Masculine and Feminine*, 1998.

Braden, Gregg, *Resilience from the Heart: The Power to Thrive in Life's Extremes*, 2014.

Brown, Michael, *The Presence Process: A Journey into Present Moment Awareness*, 2010.

Desjardins, Arnaud, *Ever Present Peace: Psychological and Spiritual Health*, 2018.

Devaki Ma, *Nectar Drops*, 2018.

Fox, Matthew, *Original Blessing*, 1983.

Gilbert, Elizabeth, *Big Magic: Creative Living Beyond Fear*, 2015.

Hollis, James, *Finding Meaning in the Second Half of Life: How to Finally, Really Grow Up*, 2005.

———, *Living Between Worlds: Finding Personal Resilience in Changing Times*, 2020.

Johnson, Robert, *Owning Your Own Shadow: Understanding the Dark Side of the Psyche*, 1991.

Jung, C.G., *Memories, Dreams, Reflections*, revised edition, 1989.

Kimmerer, Robin Wall, *Braiding Sweetgrass: Indigenous Wisdom, Scientific Knowledge, and the Teachings of Plants*, 2013.

Lozowick, Lee & M. Young, *Enlightened Duality: Essays on Art, Beauty, Life, and Reality As It Is*, 2009.

Macy, Joanna, *A Wild Love for the World*, 2020.

Meade, Michael, *Awakening the Soul: A Deep Response to a Troubled World*, 2018.

Merton, Thomas, *New Seeds of Contemplation*, 1949.

Mingur Rinpoche, Yongey, *In Love with the World: What a Buddhist Monk Can Teach You About Living and Nearly Dying*, 2019.

Nestor, James, *Breath: The New Science of a Lost Art*, 2020.

Powers, Richard, *The Overstory*, 2018.

Prechtel, Martin, *The Smell of Rain on Dust: Grief and Praise*, 2015.

Ramdas, Swami, *The Essential Ramdas*, 2005.

Ravindra, Ravi, *The Bhagavad Gita: A Guide to Navigating the Battle of Life*, 2017.

Red Hawk, *Self-Observation: The Awakening of Conscience, An Owner's Manual*, 2009.

Rohr, Richard, *The Naked Now*, 2009.

Ryan, Regina Sara, *Praying Dangerously*, 2011.

Starr, Mirabai, *Caravan of No Despair*, 2015.

_____, *Wild Mercy: Living the Fierce and Tender Wisdom of the Women Mystics*, 2019.

Svoboda, Robert, *Vastu: Breathing Life into Space*, 2013.

Trungpa Rinpoche, Chögyam, *Shambhala: The Sacred Path of the Warrior*, 1984.

Vaughan-Lee, Llewellyn (editor), *Spiritual Ecology: The Cry of the Earth*, 2013.

INDEX

ABOUT THE AUTHOR

MARY ANGELON YOUNG, M.S., is a writer, teacher, grandmother, traveler and seasoned adventurer on the spiritual path. With a background in transpersonal psychology and Jungian studies, she has published eleven books on spirituality, biography, and the Indian traditions with more recent forays into historical fiction with a spiritual bent. Her passion for the mythic and wisdom traditions of the world blends well with years of pilgrimage in India and Europe to make her books—and her workshops in the U.S., Mexico, Europe, and Canada—a unique and enriching experience. Mary lives in the high desert of central Arizona.

Contact: www.maryangelonyoung.com

ABOUT HOHM PRESS

HOHM PRESS is committed to publishing books that provide readers with alternatives to the materialistic values of the current culture, and promote self-awareness, the recognition of interdependence, and compassion. Our subject areas include parenting, transpersonal psychology, religious studies, women's studies, the arts and poetry.

Contact Information: Hohm Press, PO Box 4410, Chino Valley, Arizona, 86323, USA; 800-381-2700, or 928-636-3331; email: publisher@hohmpress.com

Visit our website at *www.hohmpress.com*